Worth the Risk

*True Stories About Risk Takers
Plus How You Can Be One, Too*

by Arlene Erlbach

D1166624

free spirit
PUBLiSHiNG®
Works
for kids™

Copyright © 1999 by Arlene Erlbach

All rights reserved under International and Pan-American Copyright Conventions. Unless otherwise noted, no part of this book may be reproduced, stored in a retrieval system, or transmitted in any form or by any means, electronic, mechanical, photocopying, recording or otherwise, without express written permission of the publisher, except for brief quotations or critical reviews.

Photo of Jonah (page 21) courtesy of Peterson Portraits, Minneapolis, MN. Photo of Abbey (page 59) courtesy of David Olsen, Dave Olsen Photography, Inc. Photo of Tren (page 63) courtesy of Emily Hart-Roberts. Photo of Christopher (page 89) courtesy of Jim Stucky Photographics.

This book contains many listings of Web sites. Please keep in mind that URLs change, and Web sites come and go. When in doubt, use a search engine.

Library of Congress Cataloging-in-Publication Data
Erlbach, Arlene.
    Worth the risk / by Arlene Erlbach.
        p.   cm.
    Includes bibliographical references and index.
    Summary: Discusses the value of taking risks and different kinds of risk-taking, both good and bad, and offers advice on and examples of this type of behavior and how to learn from both successes and mistakes.
      ISBN 1-57542-051-1
      1. Risk-taking (Psychology)—Juvenile literature.   2. Risk-taking (Psychology)—Case studies—Juvenile literature. 3. Risk-taking (Psychology) in adolescence—Juvenile literature.   4. Risk-taking (Psychology) in children— Juvenile literature. [1. Risk-taking (Psychology)] I. Title.
      BF637.R57E75   1999
      30'.12—dc21   98-38615
                                                          CIP
                                                          AC

Cover design by Percolator
Index prepared by Diana Witt

10 9 8 7 6 5 4 3 2 1

Free Spirit Publishing Inc.
400 First Avenue North, Suite 616
Minneapolis, Minnesota 55401-1724
(612) 338-2068
help4kids@freespirit.com
www.freespirit.com

Dedication

To Judy, who gave me this idea
over a plate of gourmet polenta.

Acknowledgments

I'd like to extend my gratitude to:

Karen Arnold
Marlene Brill
Evelyn Cruz
Ed Lasiuta
Tom Meyer
Florence Nemkovich

Contents

List of Reproducibles

"We don't know who we are until we see what we can do."

MARTHA GRIMES

Introduction

When you do something that has an uncertain outcome, you're taking a risk. Some risks are big and some are small. Some shout and some whisper. Some bring rewards and recognition, while others lead to failure and frustration. But all risks have at least one thing in common: They teach you about yourself and what you need to succeed in life.

Risks can be positive or negative. When you take a *positive* risk, you're trying something new to help yourself, others, or the world. You've considered your options, predicted some possible consequences, accepted that you might not achieve what you want, and decided that your risk is worth it. When you take a *negative* risk, you're not helping anyone and you may hurt yourself. Learning the difference between positive and negative risks, then choosing the best risks for you, is an important part of growing up.

About This Book

Part One, "What Is a Risk?" explores risk taking from many angles. You'll learn the real benefits of taking a risk. You'll explore positive risks and negative risks—and how to tell them apart. You'll discover how to weigh risks (are some better than others?) and decide if a risk is right for you. *Tip:* Thinking carefully about the possible consequences can help you decide if a risk is worthwhile.

In Part Two, "Real Risk Takers," you'll meet young people who took positive risks. Reading their stories can inspire you to think and act in a positive way. These young people coped with problems and sometimes made mistakes, but they acted to improve their lives or the lives of others.

Part Three, "Ready, Set, Risk!" is a road map for your own risk-taking journey. You'll find advice and pointers on choosing a risk, making a plan, setting your goals, and taking action. You may discover that something you always wanted to do is possible . . . or not. You won't know until you try.

Throughout this book, "Meet a Famous Risk Taker" sections give short profiles of well-known people so you can learn from what they've done. "Think About It," "Write About It," and "What Should I Do?" sections help you decide which risks are (or aren't) worth taking. Resources point the way toward finding out more. Reproducible forms help you organize your thinking and track your risk-taking progress.

Taking positive risks is an exciting way to learn more about yourself and stretch yourself. This book can help you identify risks that will benefit you and make you a stronger person. Like the people you'll meet here, you can go out on a limb, stick your neck out, take a chance, and make a difference.

Keeping a Risk Journal

As you read this book and become a better risk taker, you might want to keep a Risk Journal. Get a spiral notebook, loose-leaf notebook, or blank book to write in. Paste a photograph or drawing of yourself on the cover, if you want. You can also keep a Risk Journal on a computer.

You might want to photocopy pages 15, 17, 108, and 116 for your journal. If you make several copies of each form, you can complete some right away and store the others in a safe place for later. You might fill them out differently in six months, a year, or five years from now.

Following are some tips and suggestions for starting your Risk Journal. As you read this book, whenever you find a Write About It section, you may want to do the writing exercise(s) in your journal.

- Think about the word *risk* and what it means to you (For thought-starters, see "What Is a Risk?" on pages 5–18.)

- Come up with your own definitions of positive and negative risk taking. Do you know any positive risk takers? How can you be sure? Do you know any negative risk takers? What makes you think so?

- Leave room for surprises. Risk taking is risky because you don't know what might happen. Some surprises might be funny or embarrassing. Others might turn out better than you expected.

- Talk with your family and friends about what seems risky to you and why. Have them share their ideas about risks and risk taking with you. Tell them about risks you're considering; get their input and advice. Record what you learn in your Risk Journal.

I'd love to hear about your risk-taking adventures. You can write to me at this address:

Arlene Erlbach
c/o Free Spirit Publishing Inc.
400 First Avenue North, Suite 616
Minneapolis, MN 55401-1724

Or feel free to email me:

help4kids@freespirit.com

PART ONE

What Is a Risk?

"He who is not courageous enough to take risks
will accomplish nothing in life."
Muhammad Ali

A *risk* is defined as a "hazard" or "peril." And *to take a risk* can mean you "open yourself to the chance of injury or loss." While risk taking may sound scary, you probably do it every day, whether you realize it or not. Making new friends is a risk, for example. So is trying out for a team, speaking in front of your class, sharing new ideas, telling someone a secret, or starting a new hobby or project. These risks aren't dangerous or life-threatening, but in each case you may have something to lose. You might "lose face" if you don't make the team, or lose confidence if your attempt at public speaking falls flat. Or you might leave yourself open to criticism or failure. You don't know what to expect, and you can't be sure how things will turn out. That's what makes a risk *risky*.

Why take risks if you can't be sure things will go as planned? And why take the chance that you'll fail? Because risk taking has so many positive benefits. A risk is an opportunity to explore your talents, interests, abilities, and dreams. You don't wait for things to happen, you *make* them happen. Risk taking can help you become more open to new ideas and experiences; it usually involves trying something new, developing a skill, or striving to reach a goal. You may discover that you're stronger and more capable than you ever imagined.

When you take a risk, you may feel worried and unsure, eager and hopeful, excited and full of anticipation—or many of these emotions at once. Whatever happens, you're bound to learn something about the world and about yourself. It's up to you to decide whether it's worth the risk.

The Benefits of Taking a Risk

Choosing to take a risk shows you have strong feelings about something. You're willing to put yourself on the line in some way because you believe the outcome will be rewarding, significant, and worth the effort. For example, you might want to start a theater troupe because you love acting and being on stage. It's a risk to share your plan, get people involved, and become the driving force behind the project. You'll need to find the time and energy, and be willing to express your ideas. But in the process, you'll meet new people, earn recognition, and perhaps make your dreams come true. The benefits outweigh the risks involved.

When you decide to take a risk, you're about to do something you haven't done before. You're entering uncharted territory—the unknown. Who knows what could happen? One thing you can be certain of is that taking a risk means you're learning, stretching yourself . . . and growing.

Here are a few more benefits of risk taking:

- *You learn to set goals.* Everyone has dreams for the future, and some of your most cherished ones can become goals. What do you want to be when you get older? What kind of future do you imagine for yourself? To get where you want to go, you'll have to take risks.

- *You learn to face a challenge.* Many risks are challenges that demand strength, courage, and faith in yourself. When you believe a risk is worth it, you can face the challenge with a greater sense of optimism and confidence.

- *You explore new opportunities.* Risks can lead you to all sorts of new interests and activities. For example, you might decide to take a sign language class at your community center, where you find out about volunteer opportunities with a youth group for the hearing impaired. Soon you're volunteering weekly, which gives you the chance to practice your communication skills and help others, and you're even thinking about a future career as an interpreter. You might discover that with each risk you take, more opportunities and challenges await.

- *You learn about yourself.* Each risk you take will teach you about what you can and can't do. You'll discover more about your likes and dislikes, your talents and abilities, and your strengths and weaknesses. The more risks you take, the more you'll know about yourself.

WRITE ABOUT IT

 Taking risks helps make you who you are. To figure out who you are and what you hope to be, start a Risk Wish List. Begin by writing "I am . . ." and "I wish I were . . ." at the top of a page in your Risk Journal. Then come up with ten ways (or more) to complete each sentence. For example, in the first column, you might write "I am good at playing the piano." In the second column, you could write "I wish I were more confident at my piano recitals" or "I wish I could play jazz piano, in addition to classical." Now look at your list and think about how you can make one of your wishes come true. What steps do you need to take? Who can you turn to for support? Write your

ideas in your journal, then commit to taking the first step toward making one wish a reality. You can refer to this list when you're ready to take your next risk.

Positive and Negative Risks

What's the difference between positive and negative risks? Positive risks give you the chance to stretch yourself. You can use positive risks to express your opinions, share your ideas, and make your voice heard. Positive risks can also help you sharpen your skills, gain insight, and change yourself or the world for the better. Positive risks are . . . positive.

Examples:

- trying out for the school play
- running for public office
- entering a contest
- trying out for the basketball team
- telling a teacher you think something is unfair
- taking interesting but difficult courses or lessons
- conquering a fear

What if a risk seems positive but doesn't turn out the way you expect? What if you run for class office and don't win—does this mean your risk was negative? Not necessarily. Losing the race may be upsetting or disappointing, but consider what you've gained: You've probably polished your public speaking skills, gotten to know your classmates better, learned more about the issues that affect you at school, and maybe even impressed your teachers. You've tested yourself and proved that you're willing to meet a difficult challenge. This kind of risk makes you stronger.

A negative risk, on the other hand, is more likely to hurt you than help you. When you take this kind of risk, you may act foolishly or recklessly. You may do something risky on a dare, to prove something to yourself or others, because you're bored, or because you think you have no other choice. No matter what your reasons, you could end up hurt or in trouble.

Examples:

- doing something dangerous or illegal
- running away from home
- experimenting with drugs, alcohol, or cigarettes
- doing daredevil stunts
- shoplifting
- picking a fight
- lying to your parents about where you are and what you're doing
- driving over the speed limit

You may know someone who takes negative risks—and gets away with it. If so, you may question whether negative risks hurt you. It's possible to take a negative risk and not get caught (for example, you might shoplift without anyone knowing). But ask yourself what you've gained. Do you feel good about the risk? Happy with yourself? Proud of what you've done? Risks that seem daring and exciting—but put you in jeopardy—can make you feel bad about yourself. Plus, if you start taking negative risks and get away with them often, you may find it harder and harder to stop.

Rudolph Dreikurs, a psychologist, has studied young people who take negative risks. He discovered that these kinds of risk takers have four main reasons for their behavior:

1. *They want attention.* Taking dangerous risks is a way to get noticed.

2. *They want to feel more important.* They take risks like fighting and calling other kids names to feel more powerful and in control.

3. *They want revenge.* Negative risks help them "get back" at people who have hurt them in some way.

4. *They set themselves up for failure.* Because they believe they can't succeed at anything, they prove it by setting themselves up to fail. For example, these kids might choose not to study for a big test, and when they do poorly, this confirms their low self-worth.

Ask yourself if any of these reasons sound familiar. Are you taking negative risks for revenge, control, or attention? Do you expect yourself to fail, then find ways to live up to your negative expectations? If this sounds like you, talk to an adult you trust. With help, you can change your behavior.

Some negative risks start as a result of these words: "I dare you!" You might feel pressured to do something you wouldn't otherwise consider, or you might want to impress people. If a dare is dangerous and uncomfortable, you don't have to take it. You can say no, even if it's difficult. Don't let people push you into doing crazy things.

If you've taken negative risks in the past, you can turn them into something positive. Talk to someone you trust about what happened and how you'd like to make changes in your life. Discuss why you took the risks, what you expected, and whether you'd make the same choice again. Making mistakes is part of growing up, but you can learn from your experiences.

FIND OUT MORE

 If you need to talk to someone about your risks, or if you need advice about any kind of problem in your life, contact:

Boys Town National Hotline
1-800-448-3000
http://www.ffbh.boystown.org/Hotline/crisis_hotline.htm

Connect with this national hotline to talk to a professional counselor who will listen and give you advice on any issue.

Teen Advice Online
http://www.teenadvice.org/

Dozens of teen counselors from around the world volunteer their time at this site, sharing information and a commitment to helping others. Ask them almost anything and get an intelligent, caring response.

Risks and Consequences

Not every risk is worth it. You probably wouldn't choose to pick a fight with the toughest kid in school, give your oral report in Pig Latin, or jump into the alligator pit at the zoo. These actions have negative consequences; you gain nothing.

An important part of risk taking is weighing the consequences. This means imagining the outcome before you act. Ask yourself what good things might happen if you take the risk. Then ask yourself what bad things might happen. If you think the results will harm anyone (or anything), taking the risk isn't a good idea.

If you can't decide whether the outcome will be positive or negative, talk to a trusted adult. Ask your parents, other adult family members, teachers, a school counselor, or a religious leader for advice and guidance. Find out what they would do if they were in your position. You can learn from their successes and mistakes.

Your risks are up to you. Think them through, picture the consequences, and trust your feelings. If you feel too upset or anxious when you think about the risk, it may not be right for you now—you can always give it a try later. If you feel confident and excited, you're probably ready for your risk. Choosing the best risk takes practice.

What's Your Limit?

Simply being human limits your risks. For example, you may dream of flying like a bird, but you know it's foolish to jump off a cliff without a hang glider. Being young may limit you, too. You may want to drive a race car so fast that it breaks the sound barrier, but race cars are expensive—and you're not old enough to drive. Does this mean you should give up? No way!

When you're thinking about risks you'd like to take, keep in mind that certain laws and limitations may apply. At the same time, remember that young people can accomplish amazing things. You'll read stories in this book about kids who have stood up for themselves, helped others, and tried something new, and you may decide that you're ready to go for it, too. Ask yourself if your risk is realistic and reasonable. What will you gain from it? What do you stand to lose? Talk to other people about your thoughts, ideas, and feelings. Listen to what they have to say.

WRITE ABOUT IT

Make a list of risks you'd like to try. Include realistic risks—ones you're reasonably sure you can accomplish. Include farfetched risks, too—ones you'd love to accomplish, even though they seem impossible. Write down each risk at the top of a blank page (or make copies of the form on page 15 for your journal). For each risk:

- Write down the *best* things that can happen if you try it and succeed. You might make new friends, develop new skills, find hidden talents, earn money, help others, and gain people's respect and admiration. Most of all, you'll satisfy yourself.

- Write down the *worst* things that can happen if you try it and fail.

- Write about opportunities that may be lost if you don't take the risk. In some ways, not taking a risk is just as risky as taking one. If you don't try, you can't succeed.

What Will Happen?

- A risk I'd like to take is:

- Is this risk realistic or farfetched? Why?

- The *best* thing that could happen if I take this risk is:

- The *worst* thing that could happen if I take this risk is:

- What might happen if I *don't* take this risk?

From *Worth the Risk* by Arlene Erlbach, copyright © 1999 Free Spirit Publishing Inc., Minneapolis, MN; 800/735-7323 (*www.freespirit.com*). This page may be photocopied for individual, classroom, or group work only.

What if there's no time to think through your risk? For example, if you see someone in trouble, you may only have a split second to decide whether to help or what to do. In this case, you'll most likely have to rely on your instincts. When you follow your instincts, you trust your hunches or your gut reaction. Your instincts can help you stay out of danger or lend a hand to someone in need. The more you use your instincts, the sharper they'll become.

Each time you face a risk, it's up to you to decide what to do. Pages 17 and 18 can help you figure out if the risk is right for you. You can photocopy these pages and paste them into your journal. Anytime you're considering a risk, refer to these pages for ideas and advice.

Judging a Risk

When you aren't sure if a risk you're planning is positive or negative, this form can help you decide. Copy this page and fill it out. When you're finished, look over what you've written and see if the risk seems positive or not.

• The risk I'm considering is:

• Why is this risk important to me?

• What will taking this risk accomplish?

• Will this risk help or hurt anyone or anything? How?

• I talked to someone I respect about this risk. The advice this person gave me is:

• How do I think I'll feel about myself after taking this risk?

From *Worth the Risk* by Arlene Erlbach, copyright © 1999 Free Spirit Publishing Inc., Minneapolis, MN; 800/735-7323 (*www.freespirit.com*). This page may be photocopied for individual, classroom, or group work only.

Risk Reminder Card

You can consult this card whenever you feel pressured to do something risky or dangerous. Photocopy this page, cut out the card, and carry it with you. If you'd like a durable plastic version of this card, it's available for sale in packets of 50 (current cost: $14.95). Call Search Institute at 1-800-888-7828 and ask for the Positive Values Cards. (You can share the extras with your family and friends.)

After cutting out the card,
fold it in half.

KEY QUESTIONS	Positive Values
Is this a risky situation?	Caring
	Equality and Social Justice
Am I being pressured?	Integrity
	Honesty
How would my parents feel about this?	Responsibility
	Restraint
Is this consistent with my values?	*These values are important to me and my relationships with others.*
What effect will this have on my future?	
	Signature Date
What other choices do I have?	

Positive Values Card copyright © Search Institute, used with permission. Reproduced in *Worth the Risk* by Arlene Erlbach, copyright © 1999 Free Spirit Publishing Inc., Minneapolis, MN; 800/735-7323 (*www.freespirit.com*). This page may be photocopied for individual, classroom, or group work only.

PART TWO

Real Risk Takers

Risk:
Sticking up
for a friend

Jonah, AGE 17

Jonah loves computers and became a computer expert at a young age. He found a job in a computer store and worked as a certified Apple technician when he was sixteen. In addition to computers, Jonah loves cars. He drives a Ford Ranger and a Bronco.

When I was in junior high, I attended a small school with about ten boys and twenty girls in the seventh grade class. A group of about four boys thought they were really cool and popular. Other kids thought they were really cool, too, even though they would beat up kids and take their school folders. Some people said these kids destroyed cars outside of school. I thought these guys were obnoxious troublemakers, but my best friend Eric wanted to be accepted by them.

Eric invited the group over to his house a lot so they'd like him. They weren't really interested in being friends with him, and I knew it. They just wanted to play with his video games and other stuff.

During math class one day, I heard the group planning to smash some car windows in Eric's neighborhood. They didn't tell Eric about it. I figured they'd let Eric know when they went over to his house, if they told him at all.

Later that day, I called Eric's mom and told her about the plan so she'd send the guys home. I hoped that Eric had better sense than to go along with the plan, and he did. By the time I talked to Eric's mom, the guys had already roughed Eric up for not joining them. He was sitting outside alone, crying. But I knew that wasn't the end of it.

The next day at school, the guys teased him and called him names, but I stood up for him. Then the guys in the group started calling me names, too, but I didn't care. Sticking up for Eric was more important than being insulted by those guys. It also meant I'd be shut out by half the boys in my class, since the school was so small. Fortunately, this happened close to the end of my last year at this school, so I didn't have to put up with the group's teasing for long. Eric realized these guys weren't worth it and had just been using him. They weren't really his friends at all.

Standing by a good friend instead of keeping my mouth shut was a risk. I didn't know how they would respond—they might have beaten me up. Sticking up for Eric meant being insulted for a while by a group of guys admired by the other kids. This wasn't very much fun, but I knew I could handle it. Not getting accepted by the cool kids and being teased didn't matter much to me then, and it doesn't really matter to me now, either. I'm glad I stood up for Eric. That's what real friends do for each other. Now, five years later, Eric and I are still friends.

FIND OUT MORE

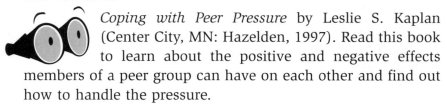

Coping with Peer Pressure by Leslie S. Kaplan (Center City, MN: Hazelden, 1997). Read this book to learn about the positive and negative effects members of a peer group can have on each other and find out how to handle the pressure.

How to Say No and Keep Your Friends: Peer Pressure Reversal for Teens and Preteens by Sharon Scott (Amherst, MA: Human Resource Development Press, 1997). This book describes step-by-step ways to deal with peer pressure without putting friendships in jeopardy, teaches you how to make logical decisions, and suggests things to do or say in specific situations.

THINK ABOUT IT

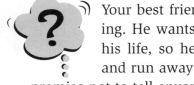

Your best friend Pete thinks your hometown is boring. He wants to take a risk and add excitement to his life, so he decides to pack a few extra clothes and run away from home—tonight. Pete makes you promise not to tell anyone about his plan. He says true friends keep secrets and stick by each other.

Is this a good risk for Pete? Why or why not? Would you tell an adult about Pete's plan? What would you say to Pete, and why?

Risk:
Overcoming
a disability

Sunni, AGE 14

Sunni loves to surf the Internet and participate in church activities. When she was in eighth grade, she won first place in her school's young authors competition and spent a weekend on a college campus, meeting writers of books for young people.

I've always loved baseball. I've watched people play the game, and I've wanted to be on a team myself ever since I was a little kid. Because I usually wear glasses and I'm blind in one eye, my pediatrician said I should stay away from sports with fast-moving objects. I was disappointed that my disability stopped me from doing something I really wanted to do.

I followed the doctor's orders for many years. Then Little League baseball started up in my neighborhood, and I really wanted to play. I begged my mom to let me join the team, and she agreed to talk to my doctor about it. He said I could play if I wore an eyeguard (protective goggles).

Joining the team was a risk. First, I didn't want to let my team down by playing poorly. I knew that I might have trouble seeing the ball, and I worried about making a mistake that could cost my team the game. I also discovered I'd be the only girl on the team, which made me a little nervous. My good buddy Joseph was on the team, too, and I hoped I wouldn't embarrass him. On top of that, the eyeguard looked kind of dorky, and I was afraid that people would make fun of me.

In spite of all the risks, I joined the team. As I had guessed, the guys weren't thrilled about having a girl play Little League with them. Some of the guys called me "eight eyes" because of my goggles. Seeing and catching the ball was harder than I thought. But I knew I'd get better with practice. I just ignored the rude comments and did my best.

I practiced throwing and catching the ball almost every day. In a few weeks, I could play as well as anyone else on the team. The guys stopped teasing me about the goggles after a while. Some of my teammates even became my friends and stuck up for me when other people teased me.

I played Little League baseball for three years. The first two years, our team placed second out of twelve teams in our area. The third year, we came in first! Winning was really exciting, but I was happy just to play and be part of the team. My risk taught me that even if things don't go well at first, you should keep trying, if what you're doing is important to you. I also learned that I can do just about anything, if I set my mind to it. Hard work can help you accomplish great things.

FIND OUT MORE

Disabled Sports USA

451 Hungerford Drive, Suite 100
Rockville, MD 20850
(301) 217-0960
http://www.dsusa.org/ ~ dsusa/dsusa.html

Disabled Sports USA is committed to providing people who have disabilities with access to all types of sports and fitness activities. More than 80 community-based chapters nationwide offer year-round recreational and competitive sports programs.

Little League Baseball

http://www.littleleague.org/

Little League's Web site includes fun activities for kids, tips for parents, addresses and phone numbers of regional offices, and more.

MEET A FAMOUS RISK TAKER

Kristi Yamaguchi was born with club feet, which caused her feet to turn in. She wore casts on her feet for a year and corrective shoes until she was five years old. Although she had a difficult time learning to walk, she still wanted to try ice skating and started taking lessons when she was about six years old. She skated so well that, by the time she was ten, she was waking up at 4:00 A.M. to practice skating for five hours before she went to school, then she practiced for two more hours after school. Her busy schedule meant she had little time to spend with friends. After she graduated from high school, she moved away from her family for further training. But all her risks paid off. Kristi Yamaguchi won the 1992 Olympic Gold Medal for figure skating and is a two-time World Champion.

Risk:
Taking an
unusual class

Frank, AGE 18

Frank loves basketball, computers, and cats. He was only a few months old when his family moved from Croatia to the United States. Frank recently moved back to Croatia, where he's studying to become a chef.

I've been excited about cooking ever since I was old enough to use the stove. I started making breakfast for myself and my family when I was only eight years old. Because I enjoy working with food, I hope to have a career in the culinary arts—I could be a restaurant critic or a chef, or I might even run my own restaurant.

To learn more about food-related careers, I signed up for a home economics class in my junior year of high school. I thought that mostly girls took cooking class, and being the only guy in the class would be awkward. Even so, I figured that learning about cooking would be worth the embarrassment. My friends thought that taking the course was a strange thing for a guy to do, but they still hung around with me and didn't say much about it.

I was surprised on the first day. Nobody teased me about wanting to cook. A few other guys had signed up for the class, mostly because they thought cooking would be easy and they wouldn't have any homework. They also liked the idea of eating the food they cooked. One other guy in the class really wanted to learn how to cook, too. He planned to go to school to be a chef after he graduated from high school.

Our first project was cherry pie. We went on to cook everyday meals, then gourmet food. I learned that cooking was more than just making something to eat—it's an art form, where you put ingredients together so they'll taste, smell, and look good.

Mrs. Nestrovich, the teacher, liked my cooking so much that she asked me to cook outside class, during study hall. Once she even had me cook a Chinese meal for more than fifty students and teachers who were studying foreign cultures. Everyone was impressed, and people told me how much they enjoyed the meal. Sometimes when I cooked and baked, I pretended to be a chef or restaurant owner.

During my senior year, I took the class again as an independent study. I was still a part of the class, but I did projects on my own and helped Mrs. Nestrovich and some of the kids in the class. By this time, I was sure I wanted a career in the culinary arts.

One day, I got a notice in homeroom that I'd won my school's Accolade Award for outstanding chef. I was the first guy to win this award. My family was proud of me, and my friends kept asking me to come over and cook for them. For me, learning about something I enjoy was worth the possibility of feeling awkward and having my friends think I was strange.

Someday, I'd like to open my own café. That's a risky business—it's a lot of work, and many restaurants don't make it. I can't wait until my friends come by to have a meal.

FIND OUT MORE

Boys Know It All: Wise Thoughts and Wacky Ideas from Guys Just Like You edited by Marianne Monson Burton (Hillsboro, OR: Beyond Words Publishing, 1998). This fun book is full of insights from boys and tackles serious issues about growing up male in America.

CookieRecipe.com

http://www.cookierecipe.com/

Like to cook? Love cookies? Check out this site for hundreds of recipes, hints, awards, a cookie of the day, and more!

MEET A FAMOUS RISK TAKER

Rick Bayless, an American, took his first trip to Mexico when he was fourteen and fell in love with the country. After studying the culture and language for many years, he took a risk and opened his own Mexican restaurant. His creative cooking style is more than just tacos and burritos—he uses his understanding of the cultures and history of Mexico to make unique dishes with traditional Mexican flavors. His cooking skills help increase cultural awareness, and his dishes taste good, too—in fact, Rick Bayless has been named "Chef of the Year" by several culinary organizations. You can look for his cookbooks at your local library.

Risk:
Filing a lawsuit

Eve, AGE 14

Eve lives with her parents and younger sister on a farm in the Berkshire Mountains. When she's not playing sports or practicing classical flute, she helps out at her parents' farm stand and works at a local bed and breakfast. Eve was featured in a CBS television special about young people making a difference.

When I started sixth grade, the boys in my class at South Kortwright Central School began to harass the girls. They called us names like "whore" and "prostitute." They felt around girls' bra straps. I put up with it until one day in October, when a boy called me an ugly, dog-faced bitch. That made me so mad that I told my mom what was happening, and she had a talk with my teacher.

The teacher didn't do anything to stop the boys' behavior. It seemed to me that the school was encouraging the behavior by ignoring it. My teacher told my mom and me that I'd be harassed all my life because I'm "so beautiful," and I'd just have to learn to deal with it. My mom even talked to the superintendent of schools and tried to have me transferred to a different class. The school refused, so I switched to another school.

Even after I changed schools, I couldn't forget how I'd been treated. The harassment had been so upsetting that I decided to file a lawsuit against my old school. I didn't want money, just an apology. I hoped my suit would keep this from happening to other girls in the future. Many of my friends, my parents' friends, and teachers at my new school told me I was doing the right thing—at first.

Not long after we filed the suit, things started to change for us. People weren't so supportive when they realized I was serious about the case. Most of my friends and my parents' friends wouldn't have anything to do with us anymore. One day at my new school, my friends wouldn't let me sit with them at lunch, and soon they stopped talking to me at all. When I went shopping, people gave me nasty looks and whispered about me. I got phone calls and letters saying I deserved the harassment. Our garage was burned down, which was really scary. Local people wouldn't buy items at my parents' farm stand. I eventually transferred to a boarding school in a different state. Even though I put up with a lot, I never considered dropping the lawsuit. I knew I was doing the right thing.

My case got a lot of publicity because not many kids file sexual harassment suits. I was suing a school, setting a precedent for future cases. My case would show that schools, like private employers, can be held responsible for sexual harassment.

During the trial, three girls testified as witnesses and described how the boys behaved. But I still lost the case. The jury thought I was overly sensitive and the boys were too young to be fully aware of what they were doing. I disagree. The boys knew exactly what they were doing, and they needed to be stopped. Harassment is never acceptable. If the boys involved don't learn this lesson now, they won't know how to treat women properly when they become adults. I'm appealing the case, and I hope to win this time.

Because of people's reaction to my lawsuit, my family will be selling our house and moving out of state. My risk has meant drastic changes for my family. But standing up for what's right has been worth it, and my family agrees. I believe that nobody should ever be harassed at school or anywhere else. I hope I'm setting an example for others to follow.

FIND OUT MORE

 *What Are My Rights?: 95 Questions and Answers About Teens and the Law* by Thomas A. Jacobs, J.D. (Minneapolis: Free Spirit Publishing, 1997). When you have questions about the law, this book has the answers. Written in everyday language, it invites you to learn about the law, consider your rights, and accept your responsibilities. Pages 124–125 cover sexual harassment.

Legal Pad Junior for Teens

http://www.legalpadjr.com/teens.htm

Chat rooms and bulletin boards for teens who want to talk about legal issues are featured here. Look for links to legal professionals who can give online advice about the law.

THINK ABOUT IT

 Sexual harassment is a form of sexual discrimination, meaning that people are treated differently based on their gender. Do you think boys and girls should always be treated the same way? Why or why not? What risks can you take to show how you feel?

Risk:
Doing the right thing

Andre, AGE 13

Andre plays on a local pony baseball league and would like to be a professional baseball player one day. He also enjoys basketball and riding his bike. His favorite subject in school is math.

I was hanging out in the park shooting baskets with Philip and Joseph, a couple of guys I'd seen around the neighborhood, when a six-year-old kid named Reggie interrupted our game. He got in the way and said we were stupid and silly, but I ignored him because I know this is how little kids act sometimes. Philip and Joseph were less tolerant, and Reggie's teasing angered them after a while. Philip grabbed a pool cue out of a nearby garbage can, and Joseph held Reggie down. They started abusing Reggie. He screamed and cried and struggled to get away. I told the guys to leave the kid alone, but they said they were just "having fun."

"That doesn't look like much fun to me," I said. Then I grabbed the pool cue, ran a few feet away, and threw it as far as I could. I believe that every person deserves respect and to be treated right. Nobody has the right to beat up anyone else.

Philip and Joseph were surprised that I took a stand and didn't go along with them. Reggie ran home, and I left, not fully realizing the risk I'd taken. Philip and Joseph probably could have beaten me up, but they didn't.

When a police officer knocked on our door that night, my mom thought I was in trouble for something. But when she heard how I'd helped Reggie, she was really proud of me.

Our local paper wrote a story about the incident, and I was given several awards. I won a heroism award from Evanston, the town where I live, and from the State Police Association. I didn't expect these honors; just helping Reggie out was reward enough for me.

Later, I had to go to court to testify against Philip and Joseph. I was scared about seeing them again in court, but they chose not to show up. The charges against them were eventually dropped because of legal technicalities. This doesn't seem right to me, but I respect the decision of the court. If I had to, I'd take my risk again.

FIND OUT MORE

Students Against Violence Everywhere (S.A.V.E.)
105 14th Avenue, Suite 2A
Seattle, WA 98122
1-800-897-7697
http://www.mavia.org/

Sponsored by Mothers Against Violence in America (MAVIA), S.A.V.E. teaches nonviolence through experiential learning while students have fun. Among other things, members have painted peace murals, presented skits on conflict resolution, and hosted forums and speakouts against violence. S.A.V.E. programs in middle and high schools are led by students and facilitated by adult advisors.

WHAT SHOULD I DO?

Q: *When I was walking home from school, I saw someone in trouble and didn't stop to help. I was worried that I might get hurt. Now I feel bad about not taking a risk and helping the person. Did I do the right thing?*

A: Sometimes it's safer *not* to take a risk. If you see a situation involving guns, knives, or drugs, steer clear and call the police as soon as you can. Police officers are trained to handle these sorts of problems safely. Helping other people is important, but your first responsibility is to keep yourself out of harm's way. Being a hero isn't worth it if you get hurt. Follow your instincts, and only step in to help if you feel safe doing so.

Take a positive risk to help work through your feelings. Find out if your local police department sponsors any programs for young people, or sign up for a self-defense class. You could also start a neighborhood watch program on your block. This can help build your confidence and make your community a safer place at the same time.

Risk:
Talking about
a tough subject

Jamie, AGE 13

Jamie, an animal lover, plans to volunteer at her local zoo. She also enjoys acting and played a soldier munchkin in a community theater production of The Wizard of Oz. *Backstage, she had the job of helping Dorothy put on her ruby slippers.*

AIDS isn't just a disease that *infects* people, it *affects* people, too. I don't have AIDS, but my mom, my uncle, and my godfather all died of AIDS. My dad has the disease, too, and I live with Sandy, my legal guardian, because my dad can't take care of me. We don't know how much longer he'll live, but most days I try not to worry about it and just enjoy the time we have.

Sandy took me in when she heard I needed a home. She's a Red Cross Certified AIDS Instructor/Educator who runs HIV/AIDS education programs as part of her job. When I first moved in with Sandy, I came along to her presentations and sat in the back of the room because I didn't want to stay home with a baby-sitter.

After hearing Sandy's presentation a few times, I decided to help her teach people about AIDS. While Sandy explained how germs infect the immune system, I drew diagrams on the blackboard to show what she was talking about. Then I told Sandy I wanted to speak, too, and let people know what AIDS had done to my family. Sandy wasn't sure this was a good idea because people might not be very nice to me if they knew how AIDS had changed my life. (This happens sometimes.) I thought about what she said, but I still wanted to help because I know it's important to teach people about this disease.

I gave my first presentation to a church group. I was nervous, but I reminded myself that telling my story could help people. I took a deep breath and talked about myself and my feelings. I shared what it was like to celebrate the holidays without my family, especially my mom. People cried. I didn't understand why, so I asked Sandy later. She said my story made a difference to them because they realized how AIDS affects real kids like me.

Sandy and I kept doing programs together, then people started asking me to speak by myself. I teased Sandy about them wanting just me, and she teased me right back. But she didn't mind because she understood how much people could learn from what I have to say.

Now I share more than just my story. I talk about how people don't have to get this disease. "AIDS is a disease of choice," I tell my audiences. "If people make good, healthy choices, they can avoid AIDS."

I've spoken to more than 3,000 people all over Kansas, where I live. I'll keep giving presentations as long as people ask me to do them. Soon we'll put my program on videotape to help even more people. I know I'm making a difference.

No one has mistreated me because of what's happened in my life. That might be because I'm a kid, but I believe no one should ever be treated badly because of AIDS. I'm glad I took my risk, because now many people know more about HIV/AIDS. People can learn how to protect themselves from AIDS—my story might even save someone's life.

FIND OUT MORE

Kids CAN!
The Kids Care AIDS Network
http://www.kids-can.org/

This organization educates kids who are concerned about AIDS and HIV. It provides guidance and assistance in finding resources about AIDS and helps raise funds to assist children living with HIV/AIDS.

WRITE ABOUT IT

Visit a hospital, hospice, or another institution that treats and cares for people with serious illnesses. Interview staff members about how they help people with cancer, AIDS-related illnesses, and other serious medical conditions. Learn about ways you can volunteer at the facility. If possible, interview a young patient and learn as much as you can about his or her condition. Keep in touch with your new friend, if you can. Record your thoughts and feelings in your Risk Journal. How can you take risks to share what you've learned?

Risk:
Saving lives

Earl, AGE 11 (left); AND
Stanley, AGE 11 (right)

Earl enjoys playing hockey and volleyball. He likes to read, and he's good at art and math in school. He hopes to work as a slasher (a person who cuts down trees and prepares logs for market) in remote Canadian forests. Stanley enjoys riding his bike and listening to rap music. His favorite sport is hockey. In school, his best subjects are art and social studies. He wants to be a police officer someday.

EARL: The risk I took was plenty scary. But I'd do it again without thinking about it.

My best friend Stanley helped me save my brother and sister from burning in a fire. It happened one snowy day in February. Stanley and I were playing hockey in my front yard. My brother Bradley and my sister Serena were inside the house, and our parents were away running errands. Suddenly, I heard

45

my sister and brother banging on the window. We turned around and saw them screaming for help.

We couldn't run to get our neighbors or anyone else. Where we live, the houses are about 100 yards apart. The closest fire department is two hours away. Stanley and I were the only ones who could save Bradley and Serena. They couldn't get out because the flames were between them and the door. I ran inside, and Stanley came with me. The house was really hot. Fire was burning the curtains. Flames spread through the house, and the heavy smoke made it hard to breathe.

Stanley and I ran back outside to throw snow all over our jackets so they'd be wet and cold. Then we put our jackets over our heads and went back into the house. We dragged Bradley and Serena outside. Fortunately, we all survived. We just had a few minor burns, and we coughed for a while because of the smoke. Within hours, our house had burned to the ground.

When I saw the fire and ran into the house, I must have known I was risking my life, but I didn't think about it that way. All I wanted to do was save my sister and brother. I'll always be grateful that Stanley was there to help me.

The Governor General of Canada, Romeo LeBlanc, heard about what we had done from our school principal and gave Stanley and me medals for our deed. We appeared on TV and received a Youth Achievement Award for Bravery. The recognition was great, but what means the most is that my brother and sister are alive.

Now I'm more confident when I try new things, even though I still get nervous sometimes. I did what I had to do, and I'd do it again.

*S*TANLEY: The day after the fire, everyone at school called us heroes. I hadn't thought of myself that way. When Earl and I went into the house to help Bradley and Serena, we weren't trying to be heroes. We saw them in danger, and we just knew we needed to save them. I'm not even sure how we got the idea to put snow on our jackets. No one had told us to do that; somehow we knew, and we did it.

Nearly everyone in our community helped Earl's family replace the food, clothing, and furniture lost in the fire. Now his family is living in a trailer until they can get another house. But they're all alive, and that's what matters most. I know that if the same thing had happened to my family, Earl would have been there for me. He would have done all he could to save us.

Because of the fire, I'm more concerned about safety now than I was before. Sometimes you don't have time to think about a risk you're going to take because things happen so fast. You don't worry about yourself—you just do what needs to be done. It's not being a hero; it's doing what's right.

FIND OUT MORE

American Red Cross Volunteers
8111 Gatehouse Road
Falls Church, VA 22042
(703) 206-7410
http://www.RedCross.org

The American Red Cross educates and trains youth and adult volunteers to help with emergency and disaster relief efforts, community education, and other needs in the communities served by individual chapters.

THINK ABOUT IT

Think about something you've done that makes you feel proud. Did you know how things were going to turn out beforehand? What did you learn from the experience? Was this a big risk, a small risk, or not a risk at all? What made you decide to do what you did? Write about your feelings in your Risk Journal.

Risk:
Starting a club

Rachel, AGE 16

Rachel loves to write poetry and stories, and sing and dance. Her favorite style of music is soft rock from the eighties. Her best subject in school is Spanish, which she'd like to teach to children someday.

Speaking up has always been important to me. If I don't agree with the way my school handles something, I'll let kids and teachers know. For example, if I think a teacher grades my test unfairly, I'll say something about it. The kids at my school didn't like that. I also made friends with some of my teachers, and many of the other students started calling me a "kiss-up."

The problem got worse over the years, and my classmates constantly called me names and made fun of me. It seemed like everything I said would be taken the wrong way. Once, I mentioned I didn't have time to take a shower, and the other kids said I had fleas. Nobody would get near me. They made up stories about me, like that I never changed my clothes, and they spread the rumors around.

Kids formed cliques just to keep me out. One boy even stomped really hard on my foot when I passed him in the hall. No one would be friends with me, except for a girl named Terri. People teased her, too. We tried to stand up for each other as much as we could.

I talked to some of my teachers, but they couldn't stop the abuse because nobody harassed me while the teachers were around. Some of the faculty thought it was all my fault. The principal suggested I change my hairstyle or wear different clothes. The counselor told me I should calm down and said that the problem was with me and not my classmates.

I knew I'd have to handle my problem by myself. In fifth grade, after I'd put up with this abuse for four years, I started a support group for kids who were teased a lot. I called it the I Don't Care Club.

I put up notices about my club in the local library, and the community column of the local newspaper mentioned it. I was afraid nobody would come to my first meeting, or that kids I knew would show up just to pick on me. I figured it was worth the risk; things couldn't get much worse. Luckily, a few kids from other schools came to the opening meeting, and we decided to meet at the library on the first Tuesday of every month. Parents came to talk to each other about the club, too.

Kids who were harassed carried a card that said "I Don't Care." This showed tormentors that we thought they were foolish and we were above this kind of behavior. Doing this was kind of risky. Some kids respected us for this, while others teased us even more. But at least the tormentors knew how we felt.

The local newspaper wrote about the club, which made the school staff angry. The teachers, and even the principal, thought I made the school look bad. They all told me that being teased is part of growing up and I should just learn to deal with it.

Kids were still mean to me—some even spat on me—but I wasn't going to break up the club. More people joined the club and came to meetings every month. After about five months, the I Don't Care Club had twenty members. At meetings, kids and their parents talked about the problem of being teased and how to solve it. We gave each other advice and suggestions, and we role-played what we might do. Newspapers, magazines, and television stations did stories about the club. *National Geographic World* wrote about it and gave the address, and I got letters from all over the world. I found out that teasing and bullying are big problems for kids everywhere. I made new friends through my club and though I still was teased, I could ignore it, knowing I had people on my side.

The teasing and bullying finally stopped when I moved to a different state. The principal at my new school says bullying and teasing are harassment and won't be tolerated. The people at my new school know about the club because an article about it was posted on the school bulletin board. Once in a while, someone will come up to me and say "I don't care" in a snotty way, but I ignore it.

I'm glad I started the club. If a kid can't avoid being teased, the club can help him or her find ways to gain support and handle the situation. Nobody deserves to be tormented all the time.

FIND OUT MORE

 Contact Rachel for help on problems with teasing or for information about starting your own club. Write to the I Don't Care Club, 420 Strickland Street, Glastonbury, CT 06033.

Bullies Are a Pain in the Brain by Trevor Romain (Minneapolis: Free Spirit Publishing, 1997). As you laugh along with the jokes and cartoons in this book, you'll learn tried-and-true ways to deal with bullies.

Cliques, Phonies, and Other Baloney by Trevor Romain (Minneapolis: Free Spirit Publishing, 1998). This book can help you learn the skills you need to make and keep friends— real friends, not people who pretend to be cool.

Stick Up For Yourself! Every Kid's Guide to Personal Power and Positive Self-Esteem by Gershen Kaufman, Ph.D., and Lev Raphael, Ph.D. (Minneapolis: Free Spirit Publishing, 1990). This book can help you learn strategies for building your personal power and assertiveness skills, as well as improve your self-esteem. A Teacher's Guide is also available.

The Ultimate Kids' Club Book: How to Organize, Find Members, Run Meetings, Raise Money, Handle Problems, and Much More! by Melissa Maupin (Minneapolis: Free Spirit Publishing, 1996). Starting a club is a great way to meet new people and make friends. This book will tell you everything you need to know to start a club and make it last.

Disney's Family Site
http://www.family.com/
An entertaining, informative, helpful site for kids, parents, and anyone who cares about young people. You can use a keyword to search for tips on dealing with bullies, safety in school, and helping other kids stick up for themselves.

WRITE ABOUT IT

Almost everyone has been teased at some time or another. Write about one time when you were teased. How did it feel? How do you think the other person felt? What did you do? What could you have done to make things different? What can you do in the future?

You could also write to several famous people and ask them if they've ever been teased, and what they did about it. (Ask your librarian to help you find an address. Or check out *The Address Book* or *The Kid's Address Book* by Michael Levine; each includes thousands of addresses for famous people, and both are updated often.) If you're lucky, you might get a response.

Risk:
Learning from
a mistake

Jorge, AGE 21

Jorge likes to play basketball in his neighborhood park. He's a youth leader at his church and will soon be traveling around the country giving speeches about the dangers of gangs.

When I was thirteen, I joined a gang because I thought it would make my life easy. I thought I'd make money selling guns, drugs, or stolen car radios. I knew people in gangs with fancy cars and nice clothes, and I thought joining a gang would make people respect me. I was wrong.

As I became more involved in gang activity, I started seeing the risks and consequences of gang membership. I went to the funerals of friends who were killed in gang fights. I visited friends who were in wheelchairs, paralyzed by gunshot wounds. Other friends ended up in jail. Still, I stayed in the gang because I thought I didn't have much of a future. I'd been a decent student in school, but my grades dropped and I failed courses after I joined the gang. I used to cut school a lot to hang out with the gang.

After I'd been in the gang a few years, something happened that finally made me realize how dangerous it was. Members of a rival gang came to our neighborhood to reclaim some turf. I was nearly killed in the fight that followed, and only one of my gang friends tried to help me. (Gang loyalty isn't all it's cracked up to be.)

After that, my mom sent me to live with my uncle Able in Liberal, Kansas. I started going to church, and I accepted Jesus Christ as my personal savior. He gave me hope. I changed my behavior because of my new beliefs, and I met people who weren't gang members. I knew for sure that I wanted to go back to school, stay away from gangs, and make a decent future for myself.

I came home eight months later. I told the gang I was dropping out and going back to school. This was risky. Sometimes people have to "walk the line" to get out, which means that the person who's leaving gets beaten up by each member, and sometimes ends up in the hospital. I was lucky; the gang respected my decision and let me go without any trouble. They've never bothered me since, and I still see some of them every so often.

Now I'm back in school, and I'm planning to go to college to become a social worker. For the last four years, I've worked for Youth for Christ as a gang counselor. I also work on an anti-gang project at the University of Chicago. I tell kids, "You've got better things to do than join a gang. It's never too early to start thinking about your future."

I took a risk when I joined the gang and another risk when I left. Leaving the gang made me realize that I can do something important with my life—I can help kids who are dealing with the same problems I faced.

FIND OUT MORE

Boys & Girls Clubs of America
1230 West Peachtree Street, NW
Atlanta, GA 30309
(404) 815-5700
http://www.bgca.org/

It's important for young people to have caring, concerned adults in their lives. Boys & Girls Clubs offer that—and more.

Tookie's Corner
http://www.tookie.com

This anti-gang site includes words of caution from prison inmate Stanley "Tookie" Williams, cofounder of the Crips gang.

THINK ABOUT IT

Think about a negative risk you've taken, and why. Now think about a positive risk you could take to help others learn from your mistake. If you got in a fight at school, for example, talk to a teacher about ways you might help settle disputes between classmates. Share your knowledge with other students.

Risk:
Inventing and
selling a product

Abbey, AGE 12

Abbey enjoys skiing and is in the master's program at her skiing school. She lives with her parents and two younger sisters, and has traveled with them to Europe and Africa. Her family is growing—she'll soon have two new siblings from Ethiopia.

My dad was cooking bacon in the microwave one Saturday morning and ran out of paper towels to sop up the grease. Then I had an idea: If he drip-dried the bacon over a dish, the grease would fall right off and he wouldn't need to use any paper towels at all.

I'd created things for school invention fairs before, but this seemed like an especially useful invention. Together, my dad and I designed a dish for cooking bacon in the microwave, which we trademarked Makin Bacon®. This dish is a small plastic tray with a handle, with three small T-shaped hangers for holding the bacon. The grease drips off the bacon and into the dish.

Inventing anything and trying to sell it is a risk. We placed an ad on the back of bacon packages and ran commercials on TV. Many people thought my idea was a good one.

Producing my invention was an even bigger risk for my family and me. We paid thousands of dollars to a manufacturing company to make hundreds of thousands of Makin Bacon dishes to fill orders we'd received. To get the money, we mortgaged our house and my grandfather's farm. Fortunately, we've made enough to pay back the loans, and more. I've sold more than a million dishes now. All kinds of magazines, including *People*, wrote stories about my idea.

Because of my product, I had to take another risk—I sued a company that tried to steal my invention. Not long after a story about my invention ran in *The National Enquirer*, a company called TriStar Products called my dad. They wanted to gain the right to manufacture our bacon cooker. They planned to pay us fifty cents for each dish they sold, and sell about a million dishes. That's a lot of money! TriStar even flew my dad to their headquarters for a meeting. The idea sounded good, but we didn't hear from them afterward.

A dissatisfied customer called us soon after the meeting. She said she'd liked Makin Bacon and bought a second cooker for her daughter, but she was disappointed that the quality had gone down. We figured out that the woman wasn't talking about our product, but a bacon cooking dish manufactured by TriStar.

Boy, was I furious—TriStar had deceived us. They stole my idea and were making and selling their own version. With the help of my dad, I sued them. Since TriStar is a big company and Makin Bacon is a small, family-owned business started by a kid, I didn't know if I had much of a chance to win the case. So far, I'm the youngest investor ever represented by the law firm we hired.

Lawyers are expensive, and the case cost thousands of dollars. If we'd lost, we would have lost the money we paid the lawyers and TriStar would have been able to continue making my product. Fortunately, we won. Before the trial even started, TriStar agreed to stop making their bacon cooker and send the mold for their dish to us. They paid us $150,000 in damages and acknowledged that I was the true owner of the patent.

Ripping off a kid's invention in a crummy thing to do. I wanted a written apology from TriStar, but I didn't get one. Still, I'm glad my family believed in my invention and helped me make my risk work.

FIND OUT MORE

 Girls and Young Women Inventing: Twenty True Stories About Inventors Plus How You Can Be One Yourself by Frances A. Karnes, Ph.D., and Suzanne M. Bean, Ph.D. (Minneapolis: Free Spirit Publishing, 1995). Reading these stories and helpful advice may inspire you to become an inventor, too.

Camp Invention
80 West Bowery, Suite 201
Akron, OH 44308

This camp for inventors is offered in many cities in the United States and provides scholarships for kids whose families are unable to pay.

WRITE ABOUT IT

 Inconvenience can spark ideas for inventions. Think about something that is inconvenient for you, or that could be a problem for a small child, someone with a disability, or an elderly person. Can you come up with an invention to make things easier? Write about what kind of risk you could take to make your invention real.

Risk:
Participating in a
dangerous sport

Tren, AGE 15

Tren likes mountain climbing, in-line skating, and hanging out with his friends. His favorite school subjects are video technology and Spanish.

I've been paddling my boat down rivers and through rapids since I was six years old. Now I can make my kayak do spins, twists, and cartwheels. To keep in shape, I lift weights, do abdominal exercises, run two to six miles every day, and paddle for ninety minutes twice a day. I've won a lot of contests, including the national championship for slalom kayaking, and I've been a gold medalist on the Junior Olympics team. I'm planning to be in the Olympics in the year 2000 or 2004.

Some people think kayaking is dangerous, but it's a lot safer if you know what you're doing. My father and brothers enjoy kayaking, too, and they've taught me to keep alert on the river at all times. Even without big rapids, the river can be challenging. The current can push the boat in many directions or even turn it over. Carefully watching how the water moves and scouting ahead for possible dangers can lessen the risk. Some things about kayaking still scare me, like plunging through a six-foot wave in a huge rapid. I always watch for hidden rocks or fallen trees under the water, then shoot straight through to avoid them. To me, kayaking is a major thrill—it's more fun than riding the wildest rollercoaster at an amusement park.

I never go kayaking alone. I make sure there's a buddy on a raft or another kayak near me. If my boat flips and I get hurt, someone is there to help me. I don't use alcohol or drugs, which can cause accidents; I get my "high" from being on the river.

In the summer, I work as a kayak support person for my dad's company, which takes tourists down the river on rafts. I paddle just a few feet in front of the raft to guide it and to rescue anyone who falls out. I've even saved a few people's lives. Being a guide can be risky for me. The raft could bump into my kayak and tip it over, and I might get trapped under the raft. Once, I damaged a muscle in my shoulder when I was stuck under a raft and pinned against some logs.

Accidents can and do happen. I've heard about people getting killed on the river. One young woman was paddling alone when her boat flipped over. She hit her head, was knocked unconscious, and drowned. Another time, a raft with a group of young people in it flipped over, and one person drowned. I'm aware of the risks I'm taking, and I use my knowledge, experience, and common sense to stay safe.

After I graduate from high school or college, I'm planning to take another risk: I'd like to live in South America, learn the local language, and work for a whitewater adventure organization. I hope to own my own company that takes adventurers on whitewater expeditions in South America.

Some people might say I'm reckless because I enjoy kayaking. But I know there's a big difference between being reckless and being a risk taker. When I'm on the river, I feel strong and alive. Kayaking is a challenge that's worth it to me.

FIND OUT MORE

American Whitewater Affiliation
P.O. Box 636
Margaretteville, NY 12455
(914) 586-2355

Dedicated to conserving America's whitewaters, the American Whitewater Affiliation provides safety information on whitewater sports and sponsors events and contests.

Outward Bound
National Office, Dept. T
R2, Box 280
Garrison, NY 10524
1-800-243-8520
http://www.outwardbound.org/

Outward Bound conducts safe, adventure-based programs that help participants appreciate the environment and increase their self-respect.

MEET A FAMOUS RISK TAKER

Snowboarding is an exciting and dangerous sport, and Steven Koch is one of the world's best at it. But even an expert can get into trouble sometimes. Koch was seriously injured when an avalanche swept him thousands of feet down a Wyoming mountainside in 1998. He lost his backpack in the fall and knew he couldn't survive without food and dry clothing. Slowly and painfully, he dragged himself to a bag of supplies he'd stashed earlier in the day. The next day, a search party found him—bruised and battered, but alive. His training, experience, and instincts helped him stay calm in a dangerous situation.

Risk:
Reporting
important issues

Beth, AGE 10

Beth is a hardworking student who stands up for what she thinks is right. She loves animals and has her own dog, Sheba. She looks forward to becoming a psychiatrist someday.

It all began with *The Moosepaper*, a newspaper I started in my classroom. Getting the newspaper going was a risk because I needed my teacher's permission to do the newspaper with my class, and I had to get other kids to help write articles. Six kids became part of my staff. Most of them gave up pretty quickly because they thought it was too much work, but I stuck with it because it was important to me.

Not long after starting *The Moosepaper*, I decided I wanted a bigger allowance. I didn't get very much, just fifty cents a week, plus extra for each chore that I did. I got fifty cents for sorting and folding a small basket of laundry, and a dollar for a big one. I'd get twenty-five cents for pulling weeds, as long as I got three inches of root.

I thought that most of my friends received bigger allowances, so I asked my mom for a raise. She said that before she'd raise my allowance, I had to prove that my friends got more than I did. I thought I could use *The Moosepaper* to find out how much other kids earned. I included a form with the next edition of the paper and asked readers to answer questions about their chores and allowance.

Kids cut out the forms, filled them out, and returned them to me. I got a total of eighteen surveys back from my fourth-grade class, and the responses were eye-opening! Boys earned an average of $3.18 per week, while girls got $2.63—fifty-five cents less, even though most of the girls did three times as many chores. Brothers got bigger allowances than their sisters, for no real reason. I thought it wasn't fair. I printed the survey results in the next issue of *The Moosepaper,* with the headline: NOT READING THIS COULD COST YOU MONEY. I knew I had to stick to the facts as a reporter, but I also wrote an editorial about the results. I wanted to make sure that nobody missed the article because I thought it was too important to overlook.

After reading the survey, my parents decided to raise my allowance, but something even better happened. My mom sent a press release about the survey to our local paper, which printed a story about it. Then the article got national attention. *The Wall Street Journal* and *The Washington Post* interviewed me. Nickelodeon visited my class and taped a program about my survey. The National Committee on Pay Equity used some of my information on their Web site and in their newsletter.

The other kids didn't think I deserved all this attention. In fact, many of them were jealous. But this doesn't matter to me— I know that telling people about my survey had an impact.

My survey helped me discover an interesting fact. As a result, I got a bigger allowance. But more important, I hope that what I learned will change people's ideas about giving both boys and girls a fair allowance, and about giving people equal pay.

FIND OUT MORE

Journals and Newspapers

http://eng.hss.cmu.edu/journals

This Web site is an index of alternative publications, from the widely read to the underground.

National Committee on Pay Equity

1126 16th Street, NW, #411

Washington, DC 20036

(202) 331-7343

http://www.feminist.com/fairpay.htm

This organization works to promote awareness of the wage gap between men and women and people of color. Visit their Web site for some questions and answers about pay equity and an interesting wage gap fact sheet.

WHAT SHOULD I DO?

Q: *I'm thinking about taking a risk, but I'm worried that people will make fun of me. What can I do?*

A: Being anxious about taking a risk is natural, but don't let fear stop you from doing something you really want to do. See "What If I'm Afraid?" (pages 110–113) in Part Three of this book for some simple steps to help you cope.

Think about what's holding you back—why are the opinions of others important to you? What do you think they'll say? You may want to share your concerns with an adult you trust and come up with ways to respond to people who tease you.

Some people might make fun of you because they're jealous. Turn the situation around by asking them to take a risk with you. The worst they can do is say no. But maybe they'll say yes.

Risk:
Investing money

Steven, AGE 18 (center);
Jonathan, AGE 15 (left); AND
Jason, AGE 11 (right)

Steven, a freshman at the University of Arizona, enjoys football, basketball, watching the stock market, and going to movies (he prefers comedies). He'd like a career in marketing. Jonathan loves sports, especially basketball and volleyball. He's proud of his autographed baseball collection, which includes baseballs signed by Joe DiMaggio and Ernie Banks. Jason has collected snow domes for the last five years and now has ninety of them. His favorite has a golden retriever inside. Jason is looking forward to traveling to Israel for his Bar Mitzvah.

STEVEN: I'm the first kid in my family to invest in the stock market. My dad is an investor, and he's taught me to use money to make money—a lot of money. That's not always how

71

it works, though. I can also lose money in the stock market. It's a lot safer if I think about what I'm doing. I use my computer to keep an eye on the market and stay informed.

In my seventh-grade stock market club, I learned about investing by pretending to buy stock in a company and watching how the stock did. I got my first real stock as a gift a little later. Then I took a risk and invested $2,000 I got at my Bar Mitzvah. I chose companies I knew something about, like Nike, Toys "R" Us, and Disney. Most of the kids I knew wore Nike shoes, and even though I didn't get things for myself at Toys "R" Us anymore, my family shopped there a lot for my two brothers, Jonathan and Jason, and it seemed like a solid business. I'd been to Disney World, so I figured I knew a little bit about Disney. These investments have done well over the years.

I've also invested money from my summer jobs. Earning that money was a lot of work, so I'm really careful with it. I don't invest money I'm saving for something big, like a stereo system. I don't risk anything I can't afford to lose.

When I turned sixteen, I bought a Chevy Blazer and invested in General Motors. That stock has gone down, but I'm going to hold onto it until it's worth close to what I paid for it. Then maybe I'll sell it and use the money to buy things I'll need for college.

No matter how great a company is, the value of its stock will go up and down. It's important to be patient and not sell the stock when the market is down, and the stock isn't worth as much. If you panic, you can lose money instead of earning it. Knowing when to pull out can be the biggest risk of all.

JONATHAN: Like Steven, I decided to invest some of my Bar Mitzvah money in the stock market. I also invested in Disney, but I made some different decisions, too. I bought stock in Lee Jeans, which has done very well. I figured this would be a good investment because millions of people wear Lee Jeans, including me. Of course, I researched the company on my computer before I invested.

I've also bought stocks and bonds in unproven companies that have both made and lost money. Now that I'm old enough to earn money from summer jobs, I'm more careful about what I do with my money. I hate to waste my hard-earned income on a bad investment. I'll be ready to buy a car next year, and I'm investing to help make that possible.

Sometimes my dad gives me advice and helps me pick stocks that should do well. If I suggest a stock he doesn't trust, he thinks I'll learn from my gains and losses and lets me take my own risks. But he wouldn't let me put every cent of my summer income into something he didn't think would work. He says, "You'll learn by winning and losing—but try not to lose too much." Of course, if you study the market and the companies, you'll be more successful. I've learned a lot from investing, and I'm glad I do it.

JASON: I've been watching Steven and Jonathan invest, and I'd like to try it, too. I'll start buying stock when I have my own Bar Mitzvah money. I like bicycles and fishing, so those are the kinds of companies I'd like to invest in.

I've made a plan and decided what I'm going to do. Like my brothers, I'll watch the market before I spend my money. It's risky to invest in companies that sell faddish products. I won't take advice from just anybody, either. When people give me advice, I'll think about what they have to say, then I'll decide for myself.

Investing can help me learn more about how to handle money, make decisions, and take risks. I've seen what my brothers have done, and I can hardly wait to try it for myself.

FIND OUT MORE

 If You're Clueless About the Stock Market and Want to Know More by Seth Godin (Dearborn, MI: Dearborn Financial Publishing, Inc., 1997). The title says it all: This easy-to-read guide will answer many of your questions and prepare you to start investing.

The Totally Awesome Money Book for Kids (and their Parents) by Adriane G. Berg and Arthur Berg Bochner (New York: Newmarket Press, 1993). This book is filled with quizzes, games, kid-friendly forms, and charts. It covers the basics of money handling (including the six mistakes that cost kids money), budgets and savings, investing, paying for college, and more.

Junior Achievement
JA New York, Inc.
107 Washington Street, 3rd Floor
New York, NY 10006
http://www.ja.org/

This nonprofit organization teaches kids about business and economics. Their classroom programs, taught by volunteers in over 100 countries around the world, teach kids about free enterprise and how to get a slice of it for themselves.

The Stock Market Game
Securities Industry Foundation for Economic Education
120 Broadway, 35th Floor
New York, NY 10271-0080
http://www.smg2000.org/

If you aren't sure where to start investing, the Stock Market Game can teach you about the U.S. economic system, the stock market, the sources and use of capital, and related concepts. Ask your teachers to sign up for the classroom program.

The Young Investor

http://www.younginvestor.com/

This site features several sections designed to entertain and educate young investors, including an investment quiz, answers to common questions, and helpful articles about money and investing. Sponsored by Liberty Financial.

THINK ABOUT IT

 Money is very important to some people. Others don't worry about it much at all. Do you think money is important? Why or why not? What kind of risks would *you* be willing to take with your money?

Risk:
Moving to another country

Miho, AGE 13

Miho plans to study psychology at an American college or university when she's older. She hopes to be a newscaster on Japanese television someday.

I moved to the United States from Japan two years ago. My father relocated here because of his job, and my mother, my younger sister Misa, and I had the choice to stay home or move, too. I could have lived with relatives in Japan, but I chose to take a risk with the rest of my family and spend a few years in a foreign country. I'll be here for another two years.

Coming to a new country was very scary. No one in my family spoke any English, and we were unfamiliar with American culture. Our parents let Misa and I choose between an American public school and a Japanese private school. Both Misa and I decided to go to Ivy Hall Middle School, the public school, and immerse ourselves in American culture.

At first, I cried every day after school because I felt sorry for myself. I even felt sorry for the nice girls who were trying to make friends with me at school. I felt stupid because I couldn't speak English. The teacher didn't give me homework because she knew I couldn't do it. I talked about my feelings with my mother and my sister, which helped.

I took English as a Second Language (ESL) classes, and I learned many new words by the end of the school year. That summer, I went to a nearby sports camp to meet new people and have fun. I made friends with the only other Japanese girl there, and she helped me with my English, too.

When I went back to school in the fall, I knew enough English to understand most of what was happening around me. I still had a hard time because making friends was a struggle for me. I spent many extra hours doing homework because I had trouble understanding the assignments and translating my thoughts into English. But I never stopped trying.

After a year, Misa decided to switch to the Japanese school, where all the teachers and students spoke Japanese—she wouldn't have to learn English anymore. Making friends was easier for her there, so Misa's decision made her happy. I could have switched schools, too, but I chose to stay where I was. I knew that adjusting to a foreign culture might take a long time, and I didn't want to give up.

I'm glad I stayed at the American school, even though this choice was risky. My English is pretty good now. I've adjusted in many ways. I'm learning more about American culture, and I'm starting to feel like one of the crowd.

The culture at my school still feels new to me, though. In Japan, teachers and students have a different relationship than they do in America—no student would talk back to a teacher, and your teacher is your friend and may even come to your home. In a way, the teachers and students in Japan are on the same level, and they work on learning together as a team. Last summer, one of my teachers from Japan visited me in the United

States. We went sightseeing and had a fun time together. I don't know if many American teachers and students would do that.

I'm glad I took the risk to come to the United States, instead of staying home where things were safe and familiar. I've learned so much about myself and the world. During my time here, I've met new people, tried new food, and learned a second language. None of it has been easy, but I know this risk was right for me. I'll miss my American friends when I return to Japan. But someday I'll be back, probably for college.

FIND OUT MORE

The Web of Culture

http://www.worldculture.com/

This site can help you learn about the cuisines, currencies, gestures, holidays, languages, religions, and books of other countries.

WRITE ABOUT IT

Think about a place you'd like to travel. In your Risk Journal, write down what you know about this place, and find out more at the library or on the Internet. What language is spoken at the place you're thinking of? Learn a few words and phrases, and write them down. Contact the tourism bureau or a government office and let them know you'd like to find a pen pal who's around your age—if they can't help you, they'll probably be able to point you in the right direction. Or contact International Pen Friends, P.O. Box 290065, Brooklyn, NY 11229. Toll-free phone number: 1-800-789-4988. Web site: *http://www.global-homebiz.com/ipf.html*

Keep copies of the letters you send and receive in your journal. You'll find out more about another place when you hear about it from someone who lives there (and you'll make a new friend).

Risk:
Leaving a religious group

David, AGE 18

David has enjoyed building and fixing things ever since he was a child, and he'd like to build his own house someday. He is in the National Guard and plans to enter the Army after he graduates from college.

I was brought up in a religious group called the Church of Bible Understanding. My parents joined about a year after they were married, and my dad left when I was very young. I didn't choose to join the group; I was born into it.

The church members live together (about thirty people to a house) and follow strict rules. One rule is that children should respect their parents at all times. This sounds like a good thing, but the group demands much more than a normal amount of respect. For example, if my mom told me to go to bed and I wanted to stay up, she might tell the brothers—the adult male leaders—of the church. Then I'd get spanked with a strap. Once, my little brother was beaten so badly that he had black-and-blue marks all over his legs.

The rules of the church became even more strict when my brother was nine and I was eleven. Our pastor, the leader of the church, said we couldn't watch TV anymore. Everyone who had a television set had to throw it away. Mine was tossed down the stairs. Kids couldn't play football or do anything fun, like go to the mall or watch movies.

The kids from the church attended a parochial school but couldn't make many close friends outside the church. I felt like I lived two lives: one with the kids from school who watched TV and did normal things, and the other isolated, restrictive life with the church.

Occasionally, I was able to visit my friend Jacque from school. We went to the mall and watched movies and television together. Jacque's mom realized that I had an unusual way of life, and she listened whenever I wanted to talk about it. I knew she was concerned, but she let me sort things out on my own.

When I became a junior in high school, the church decided that everyone my age should be home-schooled, and I was taken out of the parochial school. The home-schooling was very sporadic. Most of the time, I worked with the brothers on construction jobs instead of schoolwork. I wanted a regular education and a normal life, but I wasn't sure how to get it. One day, I decided to do something about it—I just walked out. I left the church and my home and went to Jacque's house to live.

The church trusted me because I was born into it. They didn't think I'd develop ideas of my own or think of leaving. My decision was so unexpected that it took them a while to find me. The next day, my mom and a brother showed up and tried to drag me into their van. We yelled and screamed at each other for a few hours until they finally left without me. I realized I'd permanently broken my association with the church and my bond with my mother, and I could never go back. This was really difficult, but I knew I had to do it.

A few days later, I contacted an organization called The Door, which helps kids become emancipated minors. This means I now support myself, and my mom no longer has control over me. In addition, I'm officially no longer a member of the Church of Bible Understanding.

Leaving the church meant breaking away from a familiar way of life and working to support myself while I went to school. I live with a friend and pay his family for my room and board. It isn't easy, but it's worth it to me.

I still talk by phone to my mom now and then, although she tells me my way of life is sinful. Even though I don't agree with her, I still love and miss her. I try to see my younger brother whenever I can, too. And I plan to take another risk soon—I want to help him leave the church and live the way he wants.

FIND OUT MORE

Straight Talk About Cults by Kay Marie Porterfield (New York: Facts on File, Inc., 1995). This book explains what cults are and how they work, using real life examples.

WHAT SHOULD I DO?

Q: *My best friend Anthony is in a difficult situation at home. He would probably be safer somewhere else, but I don't know what to do or say. How can I take a risk and help him?*

A: If you think your friend is in danger, get help by talking to an adult you respect. Anthony might be too frightened or overwhelmed to act on his own. Ask him to go with you to talk to a trusted adult about the situation. This could be risky because you don't know how Anthony will react. Just do your best to respect your friend's feelings and give him support when he needs it.

Risk:
Going public with
a medical condition

Heather, AGE 12

Heather lives with her mom, dad, younger sister, two dogs, two hamsters, and a cat. She's active in 4-H and has won awards for raising hamsters and guinea pigs. Heather wants to be a veterinarian someday.

When I was in second grade, I had a seizure in school. My body stiffened and shook, and I was rushed to the hospital. Because I have epilepsy, I know these seizures will happen once in a while.

I stayed home for about a week after the seizure, and kids avoided me when I came back to school. A few kids even said I'd faked it. I heard people whispering that I had a "sick brain" or was mentally ill. They thought they could catch something from me. Some of their parents thought so, too, and they didn't want their kids to play with me.

Nearly three million people in the United States have epilepsy. It's a chronic illness in which the normal electrical flow in the brain is disrupted, leading to seizures. You can't catch this illness from someone else. Most people with epilepsy control the seizures with medication; I haven't had a major seizure since the one in second grade. I tried to talk about epilepsy with other kids so they'd understand it and not avoid me.

We thought people might be more accepting if they read about my illness, so my mom and I looked for books about epilepsy written for or by a child. We couldn't find a single one, so I decided to write my own book. I spent the summer writing and illustrating *Living With Seizures*. It explains what epilepsy is and how I feel about it.

Anyone who tries to get a book published risks rejection. I sent my book to forty publishers, and they all turned it down. The publishers said the book was good, but the market was too narrow. So my parents helped me self-publish my book. They invested $7,500 to have 10,000 copies of the book printed and bound. We priced the book at $7.95, and we've just about earned back our investment. The Epilepsy Foundation even recommended my book in their catalog.

Living With Seizures got lots of media attention. I was on TV, and I was interviewed for *Women's World* magazine. I signed copies of my book at a bookstore. Still, the kids at school wouldn't be friends with me. Once they knew more about my condition, the teasing unexpectedly worsened. Many of my classmates were jealous of the attention I was getting and said they were sick of hearing about my book.

Despite what the other kids said, I know publishing my book was the right thing to do. Children and adults have sent me letters saying I did a good job of explaining epilepsy and sharing my feelings. About seventy-five young children with epilepsy have written to tell me that they carry my book with them. The editors of *Cleveland Magazine* named me one of the fifty most interesting people of the year, out of hundreds of nominees. I also received a personal recognition award from the Epilepsy Foundation.

Living With Seizures touched many kids and adults, and that means a lot to me. Taking this risk helped me learn to handle difficult times and talk about my feelings. Recently, some of the kids at school have started treating me a little better, and a few have apologized for acting so mean in the past. Now I'm in sixth grade, and I even have a best friend.

FIND OUT MORE

 If you'd like to order Heather's book and learn more about epilepsy, send $7.95 plus $1.00 for shipping and handling to Tuttle Press, P.O. Box 447, Rootstown, OH 44272. Phone: (330) 325-0411.

Friends' Health Connection
P.O. Box 114
New Brunswick, NJ 08903
1-800-483-7436
http://www.48friend.com/

The Friends' Health Connection puts people who have (or have overcome) a disease, illness, or disability in touch with others who have experienced the same condition. Go online to share your experiences and offer support.

MEET A FAMOUS RISK TAKER

Kelly Huegel was twelve years old when she learned she had Crohn's disease, an incurable illness that affects the digestive system. Frightened and confused, she searched in vain for books that might help her understand and cope with her disease. Eleven years later, she took a risk and wrote her own book, *Young People and Chronic Illness* (Minneapolis: Free Spirit Publishing, 1998), to help other young people cope with an illness and encourage them to pursue their dreams.

Risk:
Running for office

Christopher, AGE 18

Christopher has two younger brothers and a sister, as well as several foster brothers and sisters. He enjoys reading science fiction and books about history. A college freshman, he likes to hang out on campus and talk with his friends.

My high school American government teacher, John Waltner, has always encouraged students to get involved in politics. I decided to give this a try, so after researching the election laws at the county courthouse, I took a risk and ran for mayor of Hesston, Kansas, my hometown.

At first, this just sounded like a fun thing to do, but then I realized this was my chance to change and improve my town. Like most towns, Hesston needed more community involvement. I believed residents should get a newsletter about what happened at town council meetings. I thought state and federal legislators should come to speak about important issues. I also believed downtown Hesston needed more attractive stores, a restaurant that would bring in people from nearby towns, and an organization to welcome newcomers.

I knew my strongest competition would come from the current mayor, who happened to be my teacher, John Waltner. John was pleased that I had chosen to get involved, but he'd already served three consecutive four-year terms as mayor and wanted to win again.

I understood that campaigning would be hard work. I'd have to cut back my hours at my part-time job and wouldn't have any extra money for a while. I also realized voters might not take me seriously because I hadn't yet graduated from high school. Running for mayor was definitely risky, but I wanted to go for it anyway. The more I thought about it, the more I realized that I had a stake in my town and good ideas for making changes.

Out of the three candidates in the primary election, I came in second. I planned to start campaigning right away, so people would take me seriously. I hoped to earn the votes that had gone to the third candidate in the primary. I printed flyers about my ideas, and my friends and I went door to door to discuss my platform, answer questions, and explain why someone so young could do a good job as mayor.

Unfortunately, I lost the election by a small margin, and I was disappointed for a while. But then I thought about all I'd gained. I learned a lot about what I stood for and how elections work. The campaign made me realize that everyone—from politicians to residents—can help their town. You can clean up the streets or local park and organize people for a project. You can speak out about what you think needs to be changed or improved. You can have a voice.

FIND OUT MORE

Close Up Foundation
44 Canal Center Plaza
Alexandria, VA 22314
(703) 706-3300
http://www.closeup.org/

This program gives kids and adults a close-up look at how government works and increases awareness of major national and international issues. The foundation even sponsors learning adventures in Washington, D.C.

The Electronic Activist
http://www.berkshire.net/ ~ ifas/activist/

Some people say that you need connections to succeed in politics—here's where to find yours. This site includes email addresses for state and federal government officials, as well as media contacts. Make your opinions heard!

WHAT SHOULD I DO?

Q: *I'd like to take a risk to improve my town, but I'm not sure where to start. What can I do to make a difference?*

A: Talk to your friends, family, neighbors, and other members of your community to find out what they'd like to change. Do a lot of people have concerns about education? Then start a reading program for early elementary kids. If people are annoyed by litter, organize a neighborhood clean-up drive. Talk to your city government about building a playground on an empty lot for kids who don't have a safe place to play.

Make a plan and take action. Organize your friends and neighbors and get their help. Soon, you may have a small army of supporters to help make your hometown a nicer place to live.

Risk:
Joining a team

Dana, AGE 15

Dana has been involved in sports all her life. At age seven, she participated in the shot put and long jump, and won a gold medal in the hurdles at the Junior Olympics. She's a straight-A student who plans to become an obstetrician.

Football has always seemed fun and exciting to me. My dad took my older brother, Sean, and me to games, and we'd watch football together on TV. Sean played on a neighborhood football team, and I thought I'd like to do the same. At the time, I had no idea that I'd be the only girl on the team.

The program was Pop Warner football, a league that's open to people ages five to sixteen. The day I signed up, I wore a baseball cap with my hair pulled up inside it. Everyone assumed I was a guy. Later, someone said to my dad, "Your other son has signed up for the team, too." Dad didn't know what the person was talking about because he only has one son. Then he realized his "other son" was me.

My dad supported my decision to play football. He knew how much I loved the game, and he felt proud that I was on the Hanlon Park team. Turns out, I was the first girl in the state of Maryland to sign up for Pop Warner football; out of about 200,000 Pop Warner players in the country, less than 1,000 are girls.

My dad warned me that the other players might be angry when they realized I was a girl. At first, many of the other team members simply ignored me. They probably hoped I'd get discouraged and quit. I didn't care, though. I was determined to prove myself and to enjoy being part of the team.

I was the player who made the most tackles during practice. I ran more than 1,000 yards during the first half of the season. My team members realized that I could play as well as any of them. Once it was clear that I was on the team to stay, my team members accepted me.

This doesn't mean it was easy for me. I played tight end during the first year, and my coaches considered me a stand-out player. Many of the less skilled players on the team got angry with me when I succeeded. They complained that I "took their positions." When the media started to do stories about me (since I was a girl in a male-dominated sport), some of the players on the team got jealous. I kept going to practice and doing my best, though. At the end of the season, my coaches voted me Most Valuable Player (MVP).

The next year, I signed up for the team again. This time, my position was defense captain. A captain has to tell the other players what to do. I was afraid the team wouldn't listen to me, but they did. I soon earned a reputation among other Pop Warner coaches as a player to watch out for. That year, I was voted MVP again. I played the following year, too, and made eleven touchdowns that season. Then I left the team to get involved in track.

Deciding to play Pop Warner football as the only female team member was a risk, but it was worth it to me. I love football, and I wanted to be part of a team. Even though some of the guys gave me the cold shoulder early on, they eventually accepted me. I proved to myself that you don't have to accept limitations. I know my risk paved the way for other girls who want to play football, and this makes me feel really good.

FIND OUT MORE

 *The Right Moves: A Girl's Guide to Getting Fit and Feeling Good* by Tina Schwager, P.T.A., A.T.,C., and Michele Schuerger (Minneapolis: Free Spirit Publishing, 1998). Filled with quizzes, facts, and upbeat, down-to-earth advice, this book inspires girls to get—and stay—healthy and take care of their bodies.

Pop Warner Football

586 Middletown Boulevard, Suite C-100
Langhorne, PA 19047-1748
(215) 752-2879
http://www.dickbutkus.com/dbfn/popwarner/

Pop Warner sponsors tackle and flag football, and cheerleading leagues for ages five to sixteen. This organization promotes scholarship through academic team ranking and individual scholar awards for participants.

WHAT SHOULD I DO?

Q: *I'm taking a risk and learning a new skill, but it's taking longer than I thought. How can I make the time go faster?*

A: Learning something new often means practicing a skill over and over until you get it right. Be patient with yourself while you're learning. Concentrate on the wonderful skill you're building and keep a positive attitude. Wherever you are in the process, think about what you know now that you didn't know before.

Risk:
Not taking no
for an answer

David, AGE 15

David has been involved in theater since he was eight years old. He sings, dances, acts, and plays the piano and trumpet. Currently, he's part of a teen group called "Celebrations," which performs for community groups in his area.

A few months before I started middle school, I read about a terrific program called USA Harvest, which was created by a stockbroker named Stan Curtis. USA Harvest transports extra food from suppliers like restaurants, caterers, and manufacturers to agencies that feed the hungry.

Realizing that school cafeterias have plenty of surplus food, I thought my school might be able to donate unused food to people in need. I asked my middle school principal, Mr. Ulrich, if he'd like to help me make my idea a reality.

I was a little scared to talk to the principal, so I told my parents about my fears. They reminded me that the worst thing Mr. Ulrich could do was say no. And that's what he did.

He told me the school would have to follow too many health regulations regarding the surplus food. He wasn't exactly against my idea, he just thought it was too much work.

I didn't want to give up because I felt strongly that feeding the hungry was worth the effort. I decided to contact the local school board to see what could be done. I wrote letters and personally delivered them to the office of each board member and spoke about my idea at the next school board meeting. The board members gave my speech a standing ovation and approved my plan. Mr. Ulrich was pleased that I was so determined to make my idea work and that I had the persistence to see it through.

We had to deal with a lot of health regulations and make sure the food would be safe before we could make any donations. For example, the food had to be packed in plastic bags, and the school didn't have extra money to buy bags. I solved the problem by writing to companies that manufactured or supplied plastic bags and asked them to help. Soon after, a company called First Brands shipped me eight cases of plastic bags. Once I had the bags, I organized the school's first contribution—salad and cartons of milk. More than a year after the idea was approved, I began seeing the results. Since then, my school has made donations every week.

After my program was running, I decided to expand. I spoke to school administrators and politicians about the importance of recycling food. Now over ninety schools in Pinellas County, where I live, donate their surplus food to people in need.

I happen to live near Dennis Jones, one of Florida's state representatives. I spoke to him about motivating all the schools in Florida to donate surplus food. Together, with the help of my mom and my older sister, we drafted a bill to encourage all Florida schools, along with other food suppliers, to start food recycling programs.

I received a medal for my efforts from President Bill Clinton and First Lady Hillary Rodham Clinton. When Mrs.

Clinton gave me the medal, I politely asked her what happened to the White House "leftovers." She said, "We'll talk."

When I got home, I wrote to Mrs. Clinton and asked her the same question. A few weeks later, I got a letter from the White House that said all surplus food is given to White House employees. I'm relieved to know that the food isn't wasted.

Helping people is important to me. Every other Saturday, I pick up a food donation from a local grocery store and give it to a charity like a food bank or a shelter. Doing this makes me feel good. Food is something a lot of people take for granted, even though about thirty million Americans go hungry every day. I'm glad that I'm able to feed some of them.

FIND OUT MORE

You can start an organization like David's in your town. Call USA Harvest at 1-800-872-4366 for more information.

**National Student Campaign Against
Hunger and Homelessness**
11965 Venice Boulevard, Suite 408
Los Angeles, CA 90066
1-800-NO-HUNGR, ext. 324
http://www.pirg.org/nscahh/

Contact this organization for information on how you can help stop the problems of hunger and homelessness.

THINK ABOUT IT

Come up with some easy ways to show you care about other people. What can you do now to make someone's life a little better? With your friends or family, brainstorm a few risks you could take to help others. Choose a risk, then make a plan to take it.

Risk:
Proving everyone
has the right
to do something
they enjoy

Callie, AGE 16

Callie likes math and singing. She has been voted choir sweet-heart and ridden on their float at the school parade. In the future, Callie would like to advocate for people with disabilities and teach disabled children.

I was born with cerebral palsy. Growing up in a wheelchair, I've dealt with the stares and whispers of others my whole life. Some people think I'm mentally retarded or younger than I am because I have trouble speaking sometimes. Other people just assume that because I'm disabled, I can't do anything. This isn't true at all. I'm a lot like other kids. I have friends, and I get good grades in school. I've jumped on the trampoline in my backyard and gone bungee jumping, and I enjoy physical activities.

When my older sister, Sky, was a cheerleader at Andrews High School, she taught me about the sport and introduced me to her coach. During tryouts, the coach asked me to help evaluate prospective team members, then I became an honorary member of the cheerleading squad. At games, I rolled my wheelchair into line with the other cheerleaders, and I rooted just as loud for our team as the other girls on the squad did. The players and fans gave me a lot of attention.

The girls were really sweet at first, but some of them got jealous. Then a cheerleader's father, who also happened to be on the school board, complained about me. He thought I was a safety risk because I might get hurt by a football. I knew I was in no more danger than anyone else on the squad. He stirred up some other squad members and their parents, and some people started saying unkind things behind my back. They thought having a cheerleader in a wheelchair didn't "look good." Some people supported my right to be on the team, and some didn't.

As a result, the principal eliminated my position on the team at the end of the season. I was told that in the future, I'd have to try out for the squad like everyone else. I'd have to perform a single cheer, a group cheer, and a dance. Each part of the routine would be worth one-third of my total score. Tryouts would have been too difficult for me because of my wheelchair. This just didn't seem fair.

Instead of giving up, I thought of a way for less athletic kids like me to show their school spirit. I decided to start the Andrews High School Pep Squad. I presented my idea to the school board and the superintendent and got their approval.

The pep squad isn't just for the best-looking or most-popular kids. Anyone with passing grades who shows up at practices and games—and has school spirit, of course—can join. Almost thirty girls have joined the squad so far. (Boys are welcome, too, but none have joined yet.)

I probably wouldn't have taken a risk to start the pep squad if I hadn't been an honorary cheerleader first. Being on the cheerleading squad boosted my confidence and self-esteem. I learned how important it is to have school spirit—

and to stand up for your rights. I decided I didn't want anyone to take away my right to participate in school athletics, just because I have a disability.

FIND OUT MORE

United States Cerebral Palsy Athletic Association
200 Harrison Avenue
Newport, RI 02840
(401) 848-2460
http://www.uscpaa.org/

Many young people with cerebral palsy participate in swimming and track and field events. This association arranges competitions at national meets.

MEET A FAMOUS RISK TAKER

Because of an illness, Heather Whitestone lost her hearing when she was only eighteen months old. In spite of this, she signed up for ballet class when she was a child. Heather felt the vibrations of the music and danced by following the other students. Heather graduated from high school, went to college, and entered beauty pageants, using dance as her talent. In September 1994, she became the first woman with a disability to be named Miss America.

"What isn't tried won't work."

CLAUDE MCDONALD

PART THREE

Ready, Set, Risk!

> "I compensate for big risks by always doing my homework and being well-prepared. I can take on larger risks by reducing the overall risk."
> Donna E. Shalala

After learning what a risk means and reading about risk takers, you might be thinking about choosing risks of your own. But where do you start? Good (and not-so-good) opportunities for risk taking are everywhere. You can use your Risk Journal (see "Keeping a Risk Journal" on page 3) and review your thoughts and ideas. Look over the stories in this book. What risks seem worth it to you?

Risks can be big or small. Your risk doesn't have to win you awards or make the evening news (but you never know!). Start by setting a goal and working to achieve it. Mapping out what will happen first, then next, then later can help you feel more confident and ready to take a risk.

Setting Goals

Charles Garfield, a psychologist at the University of California, discovered that people who set goals have these traits in common:

- They solved problems instead of placing blame.

- They planned carefully and took risks confidently.

- They were able to improve on previous accomplishments.

When you set goals and reach for them, you're making your own decisions instead of letting others decide for you. You're doing things that are important to you, which can give you a real sense of accomplishment.

To set your risk-taking goals, make a copy of the Goal Planner on page 108 for your Risk Journal. Take the form and your journal with you to a quiet place where you won't be disturbed (this could be your room, a park bench, or some other place). Write down everything you'd like to accomplish in the next year. Be as complete and as specific as you can. These are your *long-range* goals. Rank your goals in order of how important they are to you, and focus on the first few for now.

Next, write about what you'd like to accomplish during the next three to five months, in order of importance. Focus on your top three or four ideas. These are your *medium-range* goals. (*Tip:* Your medium-range goals should help you reach your long-range goals. For example, if you have a long-range goal of "making the world a better place," you might have medium-range goals of "starting an adopt-a-grandparent program at school" or "teaching younger kids how to solve problems without fighting.")

Next, write down everything you'd like to accomplish in the next month. These are your *short-range* goals. Choose a few to work on right away. (*Tip:* Your short-range goals should relate directly to your medium-range goals. You might have a short-range goal of visiting a nursing home and sharing your ideas with residents and administrators. Or you could check out children's books about friendship from the library. Either of these short-range goals could help you reach a medium-range goal.)

Carry your list of goals with you in your Risk Journal and review the list often. (Every day is best.) Change and revise your goals when they don't seem right for you anymore.*

---

*Goal-setting tips adapted from *The Gifted Kids' Survival Guide: A Teen Handbook* by Judy Galbraith, M.A., and Jim Delisle, Ph.D. Free Spirit Publishing Inc., © 1996, pages 85–89. Used with permission of the publisher.

Goal Planner

Here's what I want to accomplish in the next year (long-range goals):

1.

2.

3.

4.

5.

Here's what I want to accomplish in the next three to five months (medium-range goals):

1.

2.

3.

4.

5.

Here's what I want to accomplish in the next month (short-range goals):

1.

2.

3.

Risks I can take to reach my short-range goals include:

From *Worth the Risk* by Arlene Erlbach, copyright © 1999 Free Spirit Publishing Inc., Minneapolis, MN; 800/735-7323 (*www.freespirit.com*). This page may be photocopied for individual, classroom, or group work only.

Use your list of goals to plan your risks. You might feel nervous about presenting your adopt-a-grandparent idea to a nursing home director, for example, so that's a risk for you. Planning your risk carefully and having your goals defined can make you more confident and focused. The risks you choose can ultimately help you reach your long-range goals.

Choosing Your Risk

If you're feeling nervous or uncertain about taking a risk, start small. Answer a question in class when you aren't sure you're right, or tell the truth when you'd rather not. Read a biography of someone you've never heard of. Create something, like a piece of art or a story.

When you're ready, look over your list of goals and choose risks that can help you meet them. These tips can help you pick a risk that's right for you:

- *Use your knowledge.* Think about experiences that can help you accomplish your goals. Put your talents and skills to work for you. Build on your abilities.

- *Be selective.* Which risk can you handle best? Which one seems most likely to bring good results? Decide which risks are most important to you (and which ones you're most likely to succeed at), and start there. When you conquer one risk, you may feel more confident about the next one.

- *Act now.* Decide on a risk that you can complete in the next several weeks. You might have a long-range goal of running a marathon, for example, and you know that you'll need to spend months physically and mentally preparing yourself for the challenge. In the meantime, plan smaller risks, like trying out for the track team or running a shorter race.

Fill out a Risk Planner (see pages 113–118 for more details) for each risk that seems right to you. Make a plan, then set it in motion.

WRITE ABOUT IT ———————————————————————————

When you're planning your risk, it helps to write down exactly what you'd like to accomplish and why it's a risk for you. This can set a strong foundation for your risk and help you choose a risk that will bring you closer to a goal. For example:

- *I want to report on school events for my local newspaper because I'd like to be a journalist someday. This is risky because I don't know how good my writing skills really are.*

- *I won't let the fact that I'm a boy stop me from trying out for the part of the evil queen in the school play. I'll prove that I have talent even though people might laugh at me.*

- *I'd like to change the curfew for teenagers in my town from 11:30 to 12:30 on weekends. The late movie starts at 10:00, and teens should be able to see a movie without breaking curfew. This is a risk because no one might listen to me.*

———————————————————————————

What If I'm Afraid?

Not every risk is right for everyone. Each person has his or her own set of experiences, fears, circumstances, and limitations. What seems risky to you might be fine for someone else (and vice versa). If you're afraid of water, swimming lessons would be a big risk. To somebody who hasn't sung in front of other people, joining the choir could be a risk. For many people, forming a club or organizing people for a cause is a risk. (This is even riskier if your group might ruffle someone's feathers.) Choose risks that matter to you and ones you think you can handle.

Some people are afraid of failure. Some worry about looking foolish in front of their friends. Others have bad dreams about the future. Psychologists say it's normal, even healthy, to have some fears. But fear can be a problem if it stops you from doing the things you really want to do.

When you think about taking a risk, you might be afraid of what could happen or what people might say about you. Or the risk itself might scare you. If you're afraid of dogs, the idea of working at an animal shelter might put knots in your stomach. For you, this would be a big risk.

Being aware of your fears and how they affect you can help you handle them better. Fear takes up time and energy, and it can leave you feeling tired and helpless. Once you face your fears, you're on your way to gaining more control over your life.

Confronting your fears can help them feel smaller. You can learn to face your fear and take the risks that are important to you. How? Here are three simple steps you can take to help keep your fears under control:

1. *Figure out why your fear has power over you.* Be as specific as you can. Exactly what are you afraid of, and why? You might be afraid of dogs if your neighbor's German shepherd bit you when you were little. So you might say you're afraid of being *bitten* by a dog.

2. *Decide if your fear is rational (meaning it could happen) or irrational (meaning it probably won't happen).* If your fear is rational, think about ways to lessen the possibility that it will come true. If your fear is irrational, think about why something that probably won't happen is bothering you so much. The fear of being bitten by a dog is a

rational one. To help ease your fear, learn how your local animal shelter protects volunteers. Or you might decide that volunteering at the community center would be less scary for you right now, and you'll find a different way to handle your fear later.

3. *Talk about your fears with a friend, parent, or another trusted person.* Other people might have ideas you hadn't considered before. Sharing a fear can help it seem smaller, too. Ask a veterinarian to give you some insight into animal behavior. You might talk to a parent about your unpleasant memories—the events might not have happened as you remember them. A friend who has a dog might be willing to introduce the two of you and help you learn more about dogs. You don't have to face your fears alone.

> "You gain strength, courage, and confidence by every experience in which you really stop to look fear in the face."
> **Eleanor Roosevelt**

Meeting your fears head-on is a big risk. When you feel scared, take a deep breath. Then do it again. Deep breathing can help you calm down. Instead of thinking about why you *can't* do something, come up with reasons why you *can*. Imagine yourself succeeding. Positive thoughts can help you face your fear and look forward to your challenge.

Handling your fears *takes* courage, but it also *gives* you courage. You may not get rid of your fears altogether, but you'll learn to accept a challenge and move forward despite your fears. You'll probably feel stronger and more confident than before.

WRITE ABOUT IT

Pretend your fear is a strange, wild creature. Draw a picture of your fear in your journal. Does it have pointy teeth? How many eyes does it have? Does it have wings or legs?

Interview your fear to find out why it's so scary. Write down your questions, then write down how the fear might answer them. Here are some sample questions:

- *Why are you so frightening?*

- *Where do you live?*

- *What can I do to make you go away?*

Your Action Plan

Some risks are based on instinct, but most risks take planning. The Risk Planner on page 116 can help you keep track of your risks. You might want to make several copies for your Risk Journal. Once you've chosen your risk, here are some ways to get ready for what's to come:

- *Be prepared.* Think about the skills or special knowledge you'll need to reach your goal. If you want a lead role in the community theater musical, you may need to take singing lessons. If you want to change a law in your town, you'll need to research why the current law exists. You may even write a speech and give it at your town's council meeting.

    Some risks are reasonable when you have the necessary skills, but dangerous if you don't know the basics. You may really want to jump off the high-dive board at the pool because it looks fun and exciting. But this risk might be hazardous if you haven't mastered the low board yet. Wait until you're prepared to try a risk like this.

- *Get the support you need.* Parents, teachers, and others helped many of the real risk takers profiled in Part Two reach their goals. It helps to have someone who will give you advice and support. However, some people might not understand your actions. What seems like a positive risk to you may seem silly, pointless, or even dangerous to other people.

  Because no one else is exactly like you, no one else has the same potential risks. No one else will take a risk in exactly the same way. Think carefully about your risk and be sure it's worthwhile. Standing up to people who criticize you can be hard, but if you believe your risk is important, keep working on it. Ask the people who agree with you for help along the way.

  Can you accomplish your risk on your own, or will you need help from adults? Will you need to go places by car? If you aren't old enough to drive, can an adult or older sibling take you where you need to go? Has this person agreed to help?

  Will you need to start a committee or get help from friends? Have your friends been reliable in the past?

  Will you need money to accomplish your risk? Do you have the funds available, or will you need to earn the money? How will you do this?

- *Look ahead.* Write down what might not go exactly as anticipated with your risk—and what you could do to deal with surprises. Having a plan can help you feel more confident and ready to handle whatever comes your way.

  First, make a list of the things that could go wrong. Writing down pages of consequences might be discouraging, so just stick to a few issues. Be specific. (Instead of "I could fail," say "No one might show up at my recital.")

Then analyze the difficulty *before* it happens. What could cause it? How can you keep it from happening in the first place?

Finally, evaluate your solutions. What will work, and what won't? Incorporate your best ideas into your Risk Planner. (Making colorful posters to advertise your recital might help increase the crowd.)

During your risk, don't panic if you encounter a problem you hadn't expected. Brainstorm some solutions, then try one.

* *Visualize.* See yourself taking your risks. Picture in your mind what will happen; draw the scene in your Risk Journal, if you want. Think about who will be with you and where your risk will take place. Many successful people, especially athletes, visualize regularly. Use the Visualization Script on page 117 to help you.

WRITE ABOUT IT

To stay positive, imagine your success and how you'll feel afterward. Here are some creative ways to envision your risk-taking experience:

* Paste the masthead from your local newspaper on a blank page in your Risk Journal. Pretend you're a reporter who's writing a story about the successful risk you've taken. Include pictures and captions with your article.

* Create a poem to describe how you feel about your risk. (It doesn't have to rhyme or have a rhythm; just write whatever comes to you.)

* Write a few words about your risk on the bottom of a pair of sneakers. Whenever you wear them, think about moving in the right direction to reach your goals.

Risk Planner

- My risk is:

- It will help me meet this goal:

- Supplies I need:

- People who will help me:

- Here are the steps I'll need to take, and the dates when I'd like to accomplish each step:

  1.

  2.

  3.

  4.

  5.

- Problems I might have and how I'll deal with them:

- Here's how my risk turned out:

From *Worth the Risk* by Arlene Erlbach, copyright © 1999 Free Spirit Publishing Inc., Minneapolis, MN; 800/735-7323 (*www.freespirit.com*). This page may be photocopied for individual, classroom, or group work only.

Visualization Script

Read this script a few times to get familiar with it, then relax and go over it in your mind. You may want to listen to sooth-ing music while you visualize, or record the words (be sure to speak slowly) and play them back as a guide. Before you begin, find a spot where you won't be disturbed, and get comfortable. Relax your body and take slow, deep breaths. Take as long as you need before beginning.

Imagine yourself in a special, safe place. It can be anywhere you feel comfortable and relaxed. Take a deep breath in, then exhale. When you're in your special place, you feel peaceful and calm. You know that you can return here whenever you like.

Keep that peaceful feeling and let your special place fade. Slowly, replace it with the picture of you taking your risk. Imagine the details—what will you see? What will you hear? What will you smell? What will you taste? What will you touch? How will you feel? Let the picture surround you.

Feel your body, mind, and spirit working toward your goal. Tell yourself that you can meet the challenge of your risk, and see yourself doing it. Everything you do brings you closer to suc-cess. You are confident and relaxed.

When you're ready, let this image fade. Become aware of your body again, and slowly open your eyes. Take a few deep breaths and adjust to your surroundings. Enjoy your relaxed body and your calm mind.

From *Worth the Risk* by Arlene Erlbach, copyright © 1999 Free Spirit Publishing Inc., Minneapolis, MN; 800/735-7323 (*www.freespirit.com*). This page may be photocopied for individual, classroom, or group work only.

Tips for a Successful Risk

Ready yourself to take action by making a plan and thinking things through.

Imagine your success— see yourself acting with confidence and determination.

Set your plan in motion.

Keep your plan in mind. Do you need to change directions, back up, or stop?

Lights, Camera, Action!

Keep your Risk Journal handy as you take your risk. Jot notes and reminders to yourself in it and review your plan often. Store positive quotes and souvenirs of your risks (ticket stubs, concert programs, newspaper clippings, photos) in your journal, too, to remind yourself of your progress and give you a lift if you feel discouraged.

Think positive and keep your goals in mind, instead of dwelling on problems and difficulties. You can learn to use setbacks to your advantage. If things aren't going as you planned, you might need to take a different approach. Use your sense of humor to help you through the rough times.

Be patient with risk taking. While some risks are quick adventures, others take lots of time and effort. Review your plan and see if you can find a shortcut or a time-saver. You might recruit friends to help make posters for your food drive, for example. Asking for help isn't giving up, it's smart thinking. If you can't find a simpler way to do things, try breaking down the steps in your plan. What smaller steps do you need to take before you can complete a larger step? As you finish each step, give yourself a reward (it doesn't have to be big) to keep you motivated and moving in the right direction.

Spending every waking moment on your risk will just stress you out, so plan some quiet time. Everyone needs a break now and then—take one when you need it. Don't even think about your risk for a while. Spend time with friends, play a game, or read a book for fun. This time away can refresh you and give you a new perspective on your risk.

> **"You have to have a dream
> so you can get up in the morning."**
> **Billy Wilder**

Dealing with Disappointment

Sometimes your risk may not go as you'd hoped. This doesn't mean you've failed. Maybe you need to modify, or change, your risk. Did you try to take on too much at once? Is someone or something standing in your way? Is there another approach you could take? Review your Risk Planner and any notes you made about problems you anticipated. What happened? Ask yourself what kind of changes you could make. Here are some strategies to keep in mind:

- *Write down exactly what went wrong with your risk and why.* Look back at what happened so you won't face the same problems later. If you can't figure out why things didn't work, talk about your problem with someone you trust. He or she may notice something you missed.

- *Write down what you can change.* What can you do differently next time? What do you need that you didn't have?

- *Try again.* Many successful risk takers spent a long time reaching their goals. For example, Thomas Edison tried 1,500 different filaments before finally perfecting the electric lightbulb.

- *Try a different risk.* Now might not be the best time to take the risk you chose. Take another risk from the lists in your journal. You might be able to try again later.

- *Cheer yourself up.* It's normal to feel sad or upset about how your risk turned out, and nervous about trying something else. Don't let mistakes stop you from taking risks. Focus on the positive aspects of your risk—what did you learn about yourself and other people from taking your risk? How can this knowledge help you? If you're still feeling down, watch a funny movie or spend time with a friend to help cheer yourself up. If you can't seem to shake your unhappy feelings, talk to an adult you trust.

THINK ABOUT IT ———————————————————————

 Remember a time when your plans didn't work out. How did you handle the situation? What did you learn from it? Have you ever had a disappointment that turned out to be a blessing in disguise?

Celebrating a Successful Risk

If your risk turned out just like you planned, you may feel more confident and sure of yourself. You might feel ready to tackle the next challenge. (Or you might just feel ready for a long nap.) Whatever you feel, take time to celebrate your accomplishments. Treat yourself for reaching your goal. Share the news of your success with your friends, family, and those who helped you along the way.

Some of your risk-taking successes may be more personal and private. It's okay to keep some things to yourself. Write your thoughts in your Risk Journal or just tell yourself "Way to go." Do whatever feels right to you.

After your celebration is over, you may feel an emotion you hadn't expected: sadness. You may have spent a long time—weeks, months, or even years—and a lot of energy on your risk. It's normal to feel a sense of "Now what?" You may even feel like you've lost something important.

Take time to relax and clear your mind. Write in your journal. Spend some quiet time with yourself, or talk about your feelings with someone who cares about you. Share what you've learned with others. You'll know when you're ready to move on and start taking new risks.

But what if the idea of taking another risk scares you? After all, once you succeed at something, other people might expect you to keep being successful. What happens if you suddenly feel afraid to fail?

Remember that everyone makes mistakes, goofs up, or does poorly once in a while. If you don't do something quite right the first time, try again. You don't know if you'll reach your goals when you take a risk. Let your success inspire you and give you courage for future risk taking.

On the other hand, you may feel invincible, like you can do no wrong. This is dangerous thinking. Even if you're successful, you still need to think each risk through before taking it. Let what you've learned from your risks guide you in the future.

Reflecting on Your Risk

Even attempting a risk is an accomplishment. No matter what happened, you probably:

- gained knowledge,

- experienced something new,

- developed new talents and abilities,

- discovered your limitations,

- met new people, and

- found new friends or supporters.

Talk about and write about your risk right away, when it's fresh in your mind. Even a few days later, you may forget details and your emotions may fade. Think about how taking your risk helped you grow. What did you learn about yourself? About other people? About the world? In your Risk Journal, write down at least five things you learned from your risk. Think about the positives and negatives of your risk.

You might copy this list and put it where you'll see it every day. Add to your list as you keep learning about yourself. When you feel frustrated or unsure of yourself, read your list. Recognizing what you've done can help you feel more confident and ready to face the next challenge.

WRITE ABOUT IT

Write a letter to yourself about your risk-taking experience. Be as detailed and complete as you can. Don't worry about spelling and punctuation; no one else will see this letter unless you show it to them. Put your letter in an envelope, stick a stamp on it, and address it to yourself. Give it to a trustworthy person and ask him or her to mail it to you in six months. You'll have an eye-opening surprise when the letter arrives.

Taking risks might feel strange to you at first—new things often are. But risk taking can make you more sure of yourself and your abilities. You might even become a risk-taking expert! Share your knowledge about risks with your family and friends, and help them discover the risks that are right for them.

Index

About the Author

Arlene Erlbach has written numerous books for young people. She teaches students with learning differences at a Chicago elementary school, where she also directs the school's program for young authors.

OTHER GREAT BOOKS FROM FREE SPIRIT

What Do You Stand For?
A Kid's Guide to Building Character
by Barbara A. Lewis

This book empowers children and teens to identify and build character traits. Inspiring quotations, background information, activities, and true stories make this resource timely, comprehensive, and fun.

284 pp., B & W photos and illust., softcover, 8½" x 11", $18.95

Stick Up for Yourself!
Every Kid's Guide to Personal Power and Positive Self-Esteem
by Gershen Kaufman, Ph.D., and Lev Raphael, Ph.D.

Simple text teaches assertiveness, responsibility, relationship skills, choice making, problem solving, and goal setting. For ages 8–12. (Teacher's Guide also available.)

96 pp., illust., softcover, 6" x 9", $9.95

Making Every Day Count
Daily Readings for Young People on Solving Problems, Setting Goals, and Feeling Good About Yourself
by Pamela Espeland and Elizabeth Verdick

This book of daily readings guides young people through a whole year of positive thinking and practical lifeskills. Inspiring quotations, brief essays, and affirmations encourage kids to think more deeply about themselves and their world.

392 pp., softcover, 4¼" x 6¼", $9.95

Kidstories
Biographies of 20 Young People You'd Like to Know
by Jim Delisle

These true stories profile real kids who are doing something special to improve themselves, their schools, their communities, or their world. Includes thought-provoking questions and resources for those who want to know more.

176 pp., B & W photos, softcover, 6" x 9", $9.95

To place an order or to request a free catalog of materials,
please write, call, email, or visit our Web site:

Free Spirit Publishing Inc.
400 First Avenue North • Suite 616 • Minneapolis, MN 55401-1724
call toll-free 800.735.7323 • or locally 612.338.2068 • fax 612.337.5050
help4kids@freespirit.com • www.freespirit.com